Adventures on the Ancient Silk Road

PRISCILLA GALLOWAY
with DAWN HUNTER

annick press
toronto + new york + vancouver

To my son Walt,
with love and appreciation. —P.G.

To my family,
who are always ready to support me on my journeys. —D.H.

©2009 Priscilla Galloway, Dawn Hunter (text)
Interior design by Kong Njo
Cover design by Sheryl Shapiro
Illustrated maps on pages v, viii, 50, 102, and on the back cover by Tina Holdcroft

Annick Press Ltd.

We acknowledge the support of the Canada Council for the Arts, the Ontario Arts
Council, and the Government of Canada through the Book Publishing Industry
Development Program (BPIDP) for our publishing activities.

Canada Council   Conseil des Arts
for the Arts   du Canada

ONTARIO ARTS COUNCIL
CONSEIL DES ARTS DE L'ONTARIO

Cataloging in Publication

Galloway, Priscilla, 1930-
        Adventures on the ancient Silk Road / Priscilla Galloway ; with Dawn Hunter.

Includes index.
ISBN 978-1-55451-197-6 (pbk.).—ISBN 978-1-55451-198-3 (bound)

        1. Silk Road—History—Juvenile literature. 2. Silk Road—Description and travel—
Juvenile literature. 3. Xuanzang, ca. 596-664—Travel—Asia—Juvenile literature.
4. Polo, Marco, 1254-1323?—Travel—Asia—Juvenile literature. 5. Genghis Khan,
1162-1227—Travel—Asia—Juvenile literature. I. Hunter, Dawn II. Title.

DS33.5.G34 2009   j950   C2009-902473-X

Distributed in Canada by:
Firefly Books Ltd.
66 Leek Crescent
Richmond Hill, ON
L4B 1H1

Published in the U.S.A. by:
Annick Press (U.S.) Ltd.
Distributed in the U.S.A. by:
Firefly Books (U.S.) Inc.
P.O. Box 1338
Ellicott Station
Buffalo, NY 14205

Printed in China.

Visit us at: www.annickpress.com

Contents

Introduction   vi

CHAPTER 1

The Silk Road and the Seeker: 1
    Xuanzang

CHAPTER 2

The Silk Road and the Warrior: 50
    Genghis Khan

CHAPTER 3

The Silk Road and the Merchant: 102
    Marco Polo

Afterword   155

Further Reading   157

Acknowledgements   159

Photo Credits   160

Index   161

LANDS OF THE SILK ROAD TODAY

Introduction

The Silk Road—for centuries, this name has conjured up the sights and smells and sounds of faraway lands: shimmering desert sands; icy, windswept mountain passes; the reek of camel caravans; the hubbub of marketplaces. Above all, the title has stood for the lure of soft, rustling, luxurious silk.

Despite its name, the Silk Road was not just one path. Instead, it was made up of many trade routes that ran from China to India and Egypt, through the cities of Baghdad and Constantinople and Samarkand, all the way to Moscow and Venice and other European cities. The Silk Road traveled over land and over water.

The journey was long and difficult. Part of it was by ship, powered by sails or oars. Much of it was over land, with animals and people carrying goods. The journey from China to southern India could take a year. Marco Polo and his family took three years to travel 8000 kilometers (4970 miles) from their home in Venice to the court of the Chinese emperor in Beijing.

The Silk Road linked wealthy cities, with their richly decorated palaces and public buildings, and passed through the fertile green farmland surrounding these cities. However, much of it crossed bleak and rugged country with few inhabitants. Travelers fought off bandits, went hungry and thirsty, and survived storms and avalanches. When countries along the Silk Road were at war, soldiers often stole from travelers and sometimes killed them. In the most dangerous times, journeys along the Silk Road were few, but when peace returned, the trade routes thronged with people again. So it went for about two thousand years, dating from the fifth century BCE.

This book introduces three very different men who, for very different reasons, braved the journey along the Silk Road. The earliest of them was a Chinese man, a Buddhist pilgrim named Xuanzang (pronounced Shoon dzang) who, in the seventh century, brought important religious books from India back to his home country. The second, some five hundred years later, was a Mongolian warrior and a conqueror, Genghis Khan. The third, Marco Polo, was a merchant from Venice, who traveled east on the Silk Road to the court of the Chinese emperor in the late 13th century.

You will no doubt notice there are no major roles for women in this book. Except in the case of Genghis Khan, since women had power and position among the Mongols, women in our three travelers' lives were seldom named in the records. There were no independent female travelers in medieval times, and no epic tales of their adventures. When women did travel, we have no record of their thoughts.

Over the centuries, much has moved along the Silk Road: silk and other trade goods, such as jewels and gold, wool and linen, and salt. New ideas were born along the Silk Road too: religions, such as Buddhism and Islam, spread from one country to another, as did new technologies and inventions, art, and literature. All the explorers in this book contributed a great deal to this exchange of wares and world views, affecting change that can still be felt today. Without their efforts, some religions might have died out, some countries might have remained isolated, and Christopher Columbus might never have set out for China and discovered North America.

A Note on the Origin of the Name

No one used the name "Silk Road" in any writings from our three travelers' time. The name was created by a German geographer named Ferdinand von Richtofen. Toward the end of the 19th century, he used the name to describe a loose network of land trade routes running from China, east to Japan, and west to the Mediterranean. Von Richtofen's catchy term quickly became popular and is still widely used.

The Silk Road and the Seeker: Xuanzang

In northern China, just west of Turfan, a long caravan of soldiers on horseback and wagons pulled by straining oxen snaked its way up the first steep slope of the Qoltag Mountains. Xuanzang's saddle creaked as he twisted to look back over the expedition he was leading. He was a Buddhist monk, used to a simple and peaceful life. Now he was equipped like a prince, and the burden of leading a caravan on a perilous journey lay heavily on him. He bowed his head for a moment and silently asked Buddha to help him find strength. Then he opened his eyes and concentrated on the path ahead. He had to stay alert for any signs of danger.

The group reached the summit, and fingers of bare, reddish rock seemed to reach up, beckoning the men down into the windy ravine. As they began to descend, Xuanzang's fears sprang to life. A large party of bandits on horseback blocked the only way down. Their

Drawings of Xuanzang, like this one from 900 CE, often show him traveling with animals and weighted down with books.

leader brandished a sword, its steel edge stained a dark crimson.

"We just killed every man in another caravan," the bandit chief shouted. His long, unkempt black hair was plastered to his forehead with sweat. "Prepare to die!" He swung his blade in a menacing arc above his head as his foam-flecked horse reared up, its nostrils flaring.

Xuanzang thought fast. He knew he had only a moment to save himself and his party. Taking a deep breath, he drew himself up to his full height. At almost 2 meters (6 feet) tall, he was an imposing figure atop his large mount.

"I am a man of peace," Xuanzang declared, trying not to let fear leak into his voice, "but my men will fight and they are seasoned warriors." The monk stared boldly at the bandit chief, and then at the tough-looking horsemen gathered behind him. "I see that some of you carry broken swords and empty arrow quivers. Accept our gifts and let us pass instead."

The soldiers mustered behind Xuanzang, rattling their long lances. It was their duty to defend the monk to the death. They waited tensely as the bandit chief hungrily eyed the well-stocked caravan. He raked a grubby hand through his wild hair and assessed Xuanzang's small battle-hardened army. Then he slowly lowered his sword.

"Very well," the bandit growled. "We will take your gifts and let you go on your way." He spat on the ground in front of Xuanzang's horse. "But don't think you will be so lucky next time."

Spelling and Pronunciation of Chinese Words

Most Westerners could not read street signs or phone books in a Chinese city. Even if they learned to say some Chinese words, they wouldn't be able to match the words with what they saw in print. The letters of the English and European alphabets represent sounds, but written Chinese uses symbols, or characters, to stand for a whole word or sometimes part of a word. Educated Chinese people know about 4000 different characters.

Various systems have been developed to represent Chinese words by using the English alphabet. The most commonly used system today is called *pinyin*. This book uses pinyin for most Chinese words. You can say most pinyin words the way they look, except words that contain *c, d, q, x,* or *zh*. The following examples will help you pronounce these tricky letters.

c: pronounced like *ts* in "aunts"   Empress Cixi = tsee'shee

q: pronounced like *ch* in "cheese"   Qin Dynasty = Chin, hence China

x: pronounced like *sh* in "she"   *xi* ("west") = she

z: pronounced like the *ds* in "adds"   *zi* ("son") = dzee

zh: pronounced like the *j* in "judge"   *zhong* = jong

You can use the Internet to learn more about pinyin.
One useful website is www.pinyin.info.

The captain of the soldiers counted out silver to each bandit. As Xuanzang and his caravan watched in relief, the bandits rode off. Once again, the determined monk had headed off a deadly threat without bloodshed. He might face other dangers, but his mission was too important to turn back now.

Xuanzang was a Buddhist monk who spent 16 years, from 629 to 645, traveling the Silk Road from China to India and back again. He had passed much of his early life in quiet study, but at the age of 27, he undertook this great quest. He was determined to collect Buddhist scriptures from India, where they had first been written, and bring them back to his homeland, China, to be translated.

The Early Years

Xuanzang was born around 602 in Luoyang, one of ancient China's seven capital cities, into a family of scholars who studied the works of Confucius. Confucius was a Chinese philosopher who founded Confucianism 2500 years ago. Xuanzang enjoyed reading and studying with his father. But interest in a religion from India called Buddhism was growing in China, and Xuanzang's older brother entered a Buddhist monastery. When Xuanzang was 12 years old, he earned a place in the monastery by winning a scholarship competition.

Xuanzang in Chinese Fantasy

In China, Xuanzang is a folk hero. A novel inspired by his story and written in the 16th century, called *Journey to the West* or *The Monkey King,* is still a bestseller. Children rush home from school to watch one or another Xuanzang television series. Xuanzang's story also appears in cartoons and in movies.

The Xuanzang everybody in China knows, however, is not the heroic traveler you'll meet here. The fantasy character of Xuanzang, also known as Tripitaka, is a bumbling fool. He would never succeed without the help of three supernatural beings: Monkey, Pigsy, and Sandy. The iron monkey with fiery ruby eyes usually copes with disaster. Although Tripitaka can control this creature by reciting parts of Buddhist literature, the Monkey King is the real hero in these stories, not the monk.

In this picture from a fantasy book, Xuanzang is shown with his animal-human companions.

Xuanzang lived peacefully with his brother in the monastery for the next five years, but outside the monastery, China was in turmoil. Rebels had begun fighting for control of the country, and nobody was keeping order. Farmers could not plant their fields or harvest their crops. Nobody brought offerings of food or money to the monasteries anymore.

Xuanzang and his brother considered their options. "Perhaps we should go to Chang'an," the older monk suggested. "The new ruler will likely come from the powerful Tang family, and Chang'an is the family's capital city. We will be welcomed there."

The brothers had to walk the whole way—460 kilometers (285 miles). They found food and beds at monasteries when they could, hiding from rebels when they had to. Sometimes they begged, and sometimes they went hungry, but they finally reached Chang'an.

The civil war was nearing its peak, however, and fighting raged between the Tangs and their rivals. To the monks' disappointment, Chang'an overflowed with soldiers. Night and day, the city stank with smoke from their cooking fires; Xuanzang's ears rang with the clamor of metal on metal as armorers repaired swords and lances.

Many monks had sought refuge in Chang'an, but none wanted to stay. They needed a new sanctuary that was far enough from the fighting to remain peaceful until the new ruler emerged and the country settled down again. They chose Chengdu in the western province of Sichuan. The journey to reach it was three times as long as the trek from Luoyang to Chang'an, but the monks and Xuanzang determinedly strode into their new home.

An Idea Takes Root

Chengdu was a good choice. Xuanzang, his brother, and the many other monks were welcomed into a big monastery there. In the next few years, Xuanzang's older brother became a popular preacher, and

the Tang family assumed power. The new emperor, Gaozu, crushed any remaining resistance. Xuanzang continued to study and was ordained as a Buddhist monk in 622, but he felt he had learned all he could in Chengdu. He made the difficult decision to leave his brother and return to Chang'an.

With its broad main avenues and gilded palaces, Chang'an had become the greatest city in China. Inside one

A Buddhist monk from a time a little before Xuanzang's.

Sogdiana and Its Merchants

Sogdiana was a state west of the Pamir Mountains and the Taklamakan Desert, and east of the Arab Caliphate. Sogdian merchants dominated long-distance trade along the Silk Road, making the long circuit from their homes in the cities of Samarkand or Panjikent to China and back, buying and selling as they went. Sogdiana had its own language, but most merchants also spoke several foreign tongues, probably Arabic and Chinese, possibly Turkic and Tibetan.

According to Xuanzang, half the Sogdian population were farmers, and the other half were merchants. Traditionally, newborn boys had their tongues smeared with honey to make them sweet talkers and their palms touched with glue so that they could firmly hold a coin. Boys began their education at age five and were sent to learn trading in their teens. At age 20, they would go to a neighboring city and begin life as merchants.

of the vast markets, Xuanzang was overwhelmed by more than 3000 vendors offering gold and silverware, ironwork, medicine, fresh and dried fish, live goldfish, honey cakes, vegetables, and flowers. He was curious about the foods from Persia brought by Sogdian merchants on the Silk Road. Along narrow market streets, the monk breathed in the aromas from many different restaurants, tea shops, and wine shops. He saw crowds watching the singers and dancers who entertained them.

Now 27 years old, Xuanzang was a tall, good-looking man who exercised every day to increase his endurance and stay fit. He spoke honestly and directly, which drew others to him to listen and learn. In Chang'an, he found a community of Buddhist scholars who welcomed him, and he was able to study and discuss many different Buddhist teachings. The more he studied, however, the more troubled he became.

The Buddhist holy writings available in China were confusing and incomplete. Some teachings had been passed on orally for hundreds of years before being written down; some had been translated from documents written in Sanskrit, an ancient language of India. Translations often disagreed with one another. Buddhist monks disagreed too, depending on what they had been taught.

Xuanzang spent many sleepless nights comparing documents by candlelight and finding no clear answers to his questions. Finally, he decided what he must do. He would make the grueling journey to India, where Buddhism began, and bring copies of the original Sanskrit documents back to China to be properly translated.

Once this idea took hold, Xuanzang thought of nothing else. He rushed around the city making preparations. He located monks from India to teach him Sanskrit, and he studied accounts of earlier expeditions. He spent time in the markets learning languages from foreigners. He questioned everyone who had traveled west along the Silk Road, asking about the routes, the best time of year to go, and the weather he should expect. What supplies did he need to take?

Buddhism Basics

The founder of Buddhism was an Indian prince who lived around 500 BCE. As a prince, he had lived an easy life, but he felt that life must hold greater meaning. He set out on a journey to find that meaning, and came to believe that suffering was the basis of existence. While meditating under a tree, he had a breakthrough. He felt that the way to be free of suffering and to achieve salvation, or Nirvana, was by following what he called the Four Noble Truths. He became known as Buddha, meaning "Enlightened One," and spent the rest of his life in India teaching others.

The Four Noble Truths are the core of Buddha's teachings: suffering exists, suffering has a cause, suffering can end, and there is a path to end suffering. Buddhists don't deny pleasure to human beings, but they know it won't last. This way of thinking sounds gloomy. How can anyone enjoy life? A Buddhist must learn to see and accept the world *as it is*. Only by developing their minds can people learn the truths around them. Buddhists believe that good and bad actions in time lead to good and bad effects; this is called *karma*. Finally, Buddhists believe in reincarnation, or that each soul is reborn repeatedly. Enlightenment is the goal, to free the soul from the cycle of rebirth. Enlightenment is extremely difficult to attain, and people make many mistakes along the way. A soul whose human life was evil is reborn as a lower creature, perhaps an insect, and begins once more the ascent toward higher forms of life.

Should he walk or ride? Finally, the young monk meditated for hours to strengthen his mind and spirit for the journey ahead.

Now only one hurdle remained: Xuanzang needed to ask the emperor's permission for his trip to India. About three years before, a younger member of the Tang family named Taizong seized the throne from Gaozu. Now, Emperor Taizong had thrown the land into chaos again by attacking the Eastern Turks. Before Xuanzang could ask permission, the new emperor closed the borders of China. Nobody was allowed to leave.

A Rough Start

Xuanzang was devastated. Other monks advised him to forget about going to India, but he was determined. And he soon found an ally in the weather.

Because of an early frost, the crops around Chang'an had failed. Emperor Taizong commanded all monks to move to parts of China where food was plentiful. Xuanzang saw his chance and chose Gansu Province, a narrow corridor between two mountain ranges that provided the only route west. He settled in the westernmost city, Lanzhou, which sprawled along the southern bank of the broad Yellow River, to complete his preparations. In Lanzhou, merchant caravans prepared to cross the desert. Xuanzang preached to the merchants and traders while continuing to learn their languages.

Because he didn't have imperial permission to leave, Xuanzang made the bold decision to sneak out of China. He would be a fugitive, so he could not join a caravan and take the safer route out of Lanzhou. All merchant caravans would be checked by guards and the people would have to show their letters of permission. Instead, the monk would have to cross the great Taklamakan Desert alone.

He hid by day and rode by night, headed for a border outpost on the edge of the desert. Xuanzang felt exhilarated. He was risking his life by disobeying the emperor's command, but he was also on his way to India! At the outpost, however, his daring escape came to a sudden end when his horse died.

Xuanzang took refuge in a monastery, where he prayed for guidance about how to continue his journey. As if in answer to his prayer, a guide named Banda approached him. This man promised to take the monk safely past the five watchtowers on China's border with the desert. With most of his remaining money, Xuanzang bought another strong horse and supplies. He asked Buddha to bless his journey.

Leading the horse, he met up with Banda as they had arranged. The guide was holding the bridles of two horses. A wrinkled old man was perched on one: a red horse so skinny that Xuanzang could count its ribs.

Before Xuanzang could ask about him, the old man spoke. "I'm too old to go with you," he told Xuanzang, "but I can give you vital information. I've made the crossing many times. Do what I say and you will survive. First, you must change horses with me."

Xuanzang squinted at the swaybacked roan and raised one broad eyebrow. "If I try to get on that horse's back, it will probably fall over and die," he said. "You ask too much."

For a tense moment, the three men stared at one another. Xuanzang suddenly remembered a fortune-teller in Chang'an who had said, "I see you leaving China on a scrawny roan horse." Perhaps this animal would bring him luck. He agreed to the exchange and turned to Banda, "I have little money left. I cannot pay you a high fee for showing me the way," he said.

"Then pay me all you have," answered the guide, his smile showing his snaggled, yellow teeth. For a moment, Xuanzang was reminded of a rat. He pushed the thought aside and counted out his remaining coins.

The old man slowly dismounted. "The western roads are formidable," the old man warned. "Sand streams stretch far and wide. You can't avoid hot winds or evil spirits." He thoughtfully stroked his pointed white beard and studied Xuanzang. "My best advice to you is to turn back. Don't trifle with your life."

Xuanzang gave the man the barest of smiles and replied, "Live or die, I will seek Buddha's country and search after the great Law."

"Then guard your waterskin," said the old man, "and drink sparingly. Stay away from the five towers. Above all, take care of your red horse. He is stronger than he looks, and he knows the road." With Banda's help, the old man painfully mounted his new horse and rode away.

Night was closing in. Xuanzang carefully settled himself on the roan. The creature swayed but it did not fall, and Xuanzang and Banda set off west. Hours passed as the horses plodded on. At last the guide pointed, and in the moonlight Xuanzang saw the outline of a distant guardhouse.

"Time for sleep," said Banda. "I'll wake you before daybreak. We must be far away from here when the sun rises or the soldiers will catch us." Both men dismounted.

Xuanzang scooped out a shallow pit in the warm sand. He settled himself into it gratefully and pulled his cloak tighter against the chill of the desert night. They could not risk lighting a fire. He quickly drifted into sleep.

Xuanzang jerked awake, but instinct told him to stay still. The sky was clear, the moon three-quarters full. His ears picked up nighttime sounds, some soft rustles and creaks. One horse nickered and the other replied. There! Near the sand hill to his right, he was sure something had moved. With his eyes almost closed, Xuanzang turned his head slowly to where his guide had slept.

The man was creeping stealthily toward him. Metal glinted in the moonlight. A knife! Xuanzang was filled with fury. Banda had never planned to help, only to murder him and steal everything. Xuanzang wanted to jump up and run at his attacker. He was young and strong—surely he could scare the villain away. *I am a Buddhist priest*, he reminded himself. *What if I hurt the other man or he hurts me?* He tried to let the anger go and think clearly.

Xuanzang quickly made a decision. He yawned loudly, pretending to have just woken up, and then got to his knees. He began to pray aloud to the kind god Kuan Yin: "Protect me from assassins," he cried. "Grant me a safe journey, O Compassionate One."

Banda stopped. He did not want to tackle someone as big as Xuanzang when he was awake. Checking to make sure the monk was still deep in prayer, the guide quickly untied his own horse, jumped on its back, and rode off in a swirl of sand.

Now Xuanzang was truly alone.

Lost in the Desert

Xuanzang watered his old horse, climbed on its bony back, and tried to find his way in the moonlight. As the sun rose, the only signposts he saw in the shifting sands were the occasional pile of dung and some stark white bones picked clean by vultures. His horse trudged on.

In the burning heat of the day, the air seemed to shimmer before him. Xuanzang suddenly saw ferocious soldiers, several hundred of them, dressed in fur and felt, racing toward him on camels and horses. Their battle standards flew and their lances glittered. The monk's heart pounded, and his mouth went dry. When the soldiers vanished,

Apparitions

Many travelers in the desert have seen strange sights and heard chilling noises, from ghostly figures to the din of armies ferociously clanging their shields. Xuanzang recorded such experiences in his travel notes.

Scientists can explain some of these phenomena. For instance, a desert traveler desperate for water may see a distant lake and run toward it, only to find it is a mirage that retreats as he or she advances. The bluish light of the mirage is caused by the change in the direction of light as it passes through air of different densities. Although the bluish light is real, a traveler's interpretation of it as water is an illusion.

Xuanzang saw monstrous apparitions in the mountains as well. It is easy to imagine how swirling, blinding snow and howling wind could seem like the shapes and sounds of demons to an exhausted man.

he realized that they had been demons who existed only in his mind. The traveler shook his head and urged his horse forward.

Despite the old man's warning, Xuanzang stopped to drink at a rivulet not far from the first watchtower. *Zing!* An arrow grazed his ear. "I am a priest from Chang'an," he shouted. "Don't shoot me."

Xuanzang spread his arms wide in surrender, his flowing scholar's robes stirring up tiny sandstorms. The commandant was a Buddhist, too, and wouldn't kill a monk. Instead, he gave Xuanzang shelter for the night. The next morning, the commandant showed the traveler how to reach the fourth tower, avoiding the second and the third. "The commandant of the fourth tower is my cousin," he said. "Tell him I sent you and he will help you."

At the fourth tower, the commandant's cousin gave Xuanzang a huge leather waterskin and fodder for his horse. "The Ye-ma spring is about 200 kilometers distant. You'll find fresh water there." As Xuanzang departed, the commandant warned him: "Don't go near the fifth tower."

To avoid the tower, Xuanzang had to follow a little-used track that ran parallel to the Silk Road route. But large parts of the path had been erased by sandstorms, and Xuanzang often had to guess the way. Sometimes he had to make detours. When he was sure that he must have traveled at least 200 kilometers (125 miles), he looked around nervously. Where was the Ye-ma spring? He tugged the reins, trotting the horse about 10 kilometers (6 miles) in each direction. Panic grew with each step when he could find no sign of the spring. He knew that he was lost.

With shaking hands, he held up his new waterskin to drink. The heavy vessel slipped from his fingers, and he dove from his horse to save it. He missed. The sand greedily drank the precious water, and all that was left was a small patch of dampness. The track he had been trying to follow was completely gone. Xuanzang did not know which way to go.

Dangers of the Desert

The Taklamakan Desert is surrounded by the Kunlun Mountains to the south, the Pamir Mountains to the west, and the Tian Shan Mountains to the north. Two branches of the Silk Road cross it: one near its northern edge and one near its southern edge.

Taklamakan means "the place where he who goes in does not come out." This fearsome desert could swallow whole caravans, and plenty of gold and silver has been abandoned in its yellow sands. The inner part of the desert is under the ban of *telesmat*, an Arabic word for "witchcraft" or "supernatural," and some believe those who steal the treasure will be followed by desert demons.

In April 1895, a Swedish explorer named Sven Hedin tried to cross the Taklamakan. His party had superb equipment and should not have had any problems. However, they also had a guide who purposely misled them and did not bring the amount of water Hedin had asked for. Vicious sandstorms constantly battered them. The combination of horrors almost killed them all. To save their lives, Hedin abandoned food and equipment, including his camera gear and 1000 photographic plates. A year later, he heard it had all been found after a bag of flour had burst and turned the top of a dune white, but even the top of Hedin's storage tent had been buried a foot deep under the shifting sands.

For five days Xuanzang struggled onward. By night, demons seemed to raise lights that rivaled the stars; by day, hot winds drove the sand like a stinging rain against his skin. The exhausted monk prayed in silence; his parched mouth and swollen tongue could not form words.

Abruptly, his horse changed direction, and Xuanzang was too weak to fight him. He let the reins fall from his hands. He was barely conscious when the horse stopped, lowered its head, and began to graze. It took the monk a few seconds to realize what that meant: they were in the middle of huge fields of green grass. Nearby, a pool of water reflected the rose color of dawn. Xuanzang slid from the red horse and crawled into the water, submerging his whole body.

The King of Turfan

Xuanzang rested for a day. Then he cut some grass to carry as fodder for the roan, filled his leather waterskin again, and continued on until he came to the small oasis town of Hami. When the oasis kings heard about the priest from far-off China who had crossed the great desert by himself, they came to Hami to pay their respects. They invited Xuanzang to visit their palaces and preach in their temples.

Turfan was larger and richer than the other oasis kingdoms, and its ruler, a devout Buddhist, was a powerful monarch. Rather than coming to visit Xuanzang, he sent the captain of his royal guards and 20 soldiers to bring the traveler to him. Xuanzang realized that he should accept the invitation from such an important person, even though it meant adding 300 kilometers (185 miles) and 6 days of desert travel to his quest.

The party arrived in Turfan well after dark. The king came out with courtiers and torches to give his guest a royal welcome. Xuanzang longed for sleep, but the king insisted on talking to him all night. "Stay in Turfan," he urged. "Teach my priests. Ask for anything you want, and you shall have it."

The Land of Fire

Turfan survives today as Turpan. This Chinese city lies in the second-deepest inland depression, or low place, in the world. Once called the Land of Fire, the Turfan Depression has recorded temperatures as high as 54 degrees Celsius (129 degrees Fahrenheit). A Chinese official wrote in 1933 that Turfan's streets were deserted during the day, when the wind shriveled the skin and scorched the eyes. The market often opened at night instead.

The Oasis Kingdoms

The Silk Road passed through many small desert kingdoms, each with a green oasis as its center. The oases were nourished by glacier-fed streams that began high in the mountains that formed a horseshoe around the Taklamakan Desert. This water was carried by underground systems of wells and tunnels, called *karezes*, which are still used today. In the oases, scrub grasses grew and date palms often took root, tended carefully by the people who lived there.

Even though each small kingdom was just one city and some cultivated land, the oases were important commercial centers where caravans regularly stopped. A caravan might need to gather enough food, water, and other supplies for 100 or more people and animals to use until they arrived safely at the next oasis. An important overland trading route between China and the West could never have developed without these places to rest, trade, and restock.

Over the centuries, some of the glaciers in the mountains melted, leaving the desert to devour many of the oasis towns. But these vanished cities sometimes appear again, uncovered by the winds that previously buried them.

Today, some oasis towns survive. They have become tourist destinations, like this one near Dunhuang, China.

"Your majesty is very generous," said Xuanzang carefully, "but truly, my heart cannot consent."

The king was accustomed to being obeyed, and he lost his temper. "Do not think you can leave whenever you like." He narrowed his eyes. "I could send you back to China if you don't do as I ask."

Xuanzang was horrified that his mission might end like this. "You may detain my skin and bones," the monk exclaimed, "but not my spirit!"

He sat down on the floor and refused all food and drink, even when the king, whose anger quickly faded, served them himself. After three days, Xuanzang was weak and dizzy. "When I die," he whispered, "bury me looking toward India."

"I am ashamed," the king said quietly. "Go when you wish. I won't stop you. Now, please drink some broth." He held the cup to Xuanzang's cracked lips. "If you will stay for one month and preach to my people," he continued, "I will gather supplies and equipment for your journey."

Once the king had stopped threatening him, Xuanzang was happy to stay for a month, even though he had hoped to be through the mountains before winter.

When Xuanzang was ready to leave Turfan, the king presented him with jewels, gold and silver pieces, and oxen to pull the loaded carts. He also supplied clothing, food, and drink for the journey, horses, servants, and a guard of veteran warriors.

"You have furs for the mountains and silk robes for the deserts," said the king. "If you stay at a monastery or court, I have included bolts of fine fabrics you can give to your hosts." He clapped his hands and a courtier appeared, bowing deeply.

"My captain will conduct you to the Great Khan of the Western Turks," said the king.

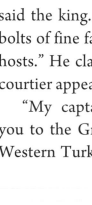

Bezeklik Thousand Buddha Caves

While waiting in Turfan, Xuanzang would have visited the Bezeklik Thousand Buddha Caves. These caves did not occur naturally; they were carved from the cliffs by hand. They were started in the fourth century and added to for seven centuries. Most of the caves have rounded ceilings covered with paintings, or frescoes. Xuanzang would have seen colorful images of Buddha—sometimes hundreds of different images in one cave. Some were obviously painted by talented artists, while others were rougher, likely created by devoted monks who lacked artistic talent. There are other scenes too, including people of different races and stations in life. Originally, these caves were used as palace temples. Later, monks lived in some, and travelers on religious missions, like Xuanzang, could rest there. In Xuanzang's time, there were many caves, but erosion and vandalism have left only about 75 today.

"I have composed 24 official letters to the rulers of the countries along the way and placed a roll of smooth satin with each letter. A separate cart carries 500 pieces of satin and taffeta for the Great Khan, along with a letter. In it, I have asked him to write letters to the next group of rulers, so that they will guide you through their lands and provide escorts and relays of horses."

For a moment, Xuanzang was overwhelmed with emotion and could not speak. The Great Khan's empire extended from Greater Khorasan and Makran west to Persia. And if the Great Khan was as helpful as the king of Turfan had been, Xuanzang would be an honored guest in every country for the rest of his journey to India. "You have been so generous," the monk said at last, cinching his wide belt tighter. "If my mission succeeds, it will be because of you."

"Will you stay here on your way home to China?" asked the king. "Stay for three years. Teach my people a little of what you have learned."

"I will do as you ask," Xuanzang promised, as he gripped the king's hands warmly. But they would never meet again. The king would die many years before Xuanzang made his way home.

What Is a Country?

Long ago, a country was not like the great nation-states that lead the world today. Most countries were small in area, population, and power. A great king might rule over many countries. For example, to the west of China, the king of Turfan was "king of kings" over 24 oasis kingdoms; in northern India, King Harsha ruled over 18 lesser kings.

Kept in Kucha

About a week into their journey, Xuanzang's caravan had the frightening encounter with desert-toughened bandits as they descended from the Qoltag Mountains. The monk managed to head off the threat without bloodshed, however, and the caravan trudged on toward the oasis kingdom of Kucha. The part of the Silk Road Xuanzang was now traveling skirted the Tian Shan Mountains. Grasses and scrub grew at the base of the mountains, softening the landscape and providing some grazing for the animals in the caravan.

Each day, the men milked the goats they had brought, but the milk supply diminished as the animals were gradually killed and eaten. The men of Turfan used every part of the goats, including the head and intestines, which were boiled to make a broth called *opke*. Nothing was wasted in the desert.

For Xuanzang, who did not eat meat, the smell of the broth and the sound of sizzling flesh roasting over the campfires were nauseating. He preferred to eat alone, consuming plenty of rice and noodles and all kinds of fruit. He particularly loved the tender melons for which the oasis towns were famous. Nothing gave him more pleasure than slicing open the delicate, fragrant fruit and letting its sweet juices wash the dust of the day from his throat.

The road was smooth, and had Xuanzang been alone, he would likely have been on the other side of the mountains by now. But the heavily loaded carts slowed progress, and it was late fall in 629 before the group neared the small oasis kingdom of Kucha. The nights had grown cold, and the towering mountains glittered sharply with packed snow and ice. The monk gazed despondently at the heights and pulled his worn brown cloak a little tighter. Because of their delay in Turfan, it seemed that they would have to stop for the winter in Kucha.

The Richness of Kucha

About Kucha, Xuanzang wrote, "grapes, pomegranates, and numerous species of plums, pears, peaches, and almonds . . . grow here. The ground is rich in minerals—gold, copper, iron, lead, and tin. The air is soft, and the manners of the people honest. . . . They excel other countries in their skill in playing on the lute and pipe. They clothe themselves with ornamental garments of silk and embroidery. They cut their hair and wear a flowing [head] covering. In commerce they use gold, silver, and copper coins. . . . The children born of common parents have their heads flattened by the pressure of a wooden board."

Kucha had embraced Buddhism a few hundred years before, and the king, too, was a Buddhist. As the caravan passed under the city gates, Xuanzang and his party craned their necks to see the towering and beautifully carved Buddha statues on each side. At the royal palace, which resembled a Buddhist monastery, the king welcomed Xuanzang with a concert by Kuchan musicians, whose playing was famous even in faraway China.

Kucha was home to at least 5000 monks, and people traveled from all parts of Asia to learn from them. Xuanzang passed his days in the monasteries, carefully recording in his leather-bound notebooks everything he saw. He described the solid, gleaming jade stone about half a meter (1.5 feet) wide in one monastery. With the permission of the old monks, Xuanzang knelt and reverently traced the outline of the imprint it held. It was said to be a mark made by Buddha's foot. Xuanzang's fingers trembled as they touched the stone, which felt surprisingly warm. Yet, even with all that Kucha had to offer, Xuanzang was impatient to continue his journey. After two months, he decided—against local advice—not to wait for spring.

The Terrifying Tian Shan Mountains

Within a few days of leaving Kucha, the travelers had entered the Tian Shan Mountains. Slowly they moved up the heights, circling a peak 7200 meters (24,000 feet) high, on their way to a pass in which the ice never melted. As they climbed, the temperature dropped and the snow deepened. It was now January, the coldest time in the Tian Shan Mountains, when the arctic winds blew in from Siberia. Xuanzang's confidence wavered and he began to wish he had listened to the people who had urged him not to leave Kucha in winter.

Every member of the caravan was wrapped in the layers of furs supplied by the generous king of Turfan, but still the bitter cold seeped into their bones. The narrowness of the mountain passageway and the relentless wind and snow meant that there were no dry places to cook food or to sleep. And then, after two days of struggling through the pass, disaster struck.

Xuanzang heard a noise like a thousand oxen galloping toward him and he felt the ground shudder. In an instant, tons of snow flowed down the mountain, engulfing the men and animals at the end of the caravan. The vibration of so many wheels and hooves had triggered an avalanche.

Xuanzang struggled to control his frightened horse, turning him around and shouting for everyone to help. Every man threw himself into the pile of snow, desperate to find those who had been buried. Their frozen hands made digging difficult, and the swiftness of the avalanche had made it impossible to tell where the other men had been swept.

Xuanzang's hand finally touched a cart's wheel. He dug furiously, his breath a plume of steam that frosted his mustache with ice. Abruptly, he pulled the wheel lose and saw that he held only a small section in his hand. The cart had been smashed into hundreds of pieces by the weight of the snow and ice. Xuanzang sadly understood that they would not find anyone alive. He could not risk the lives of the rest of his people by lingering here. He told the exhausted men to stop searching. They reluctantly fell back.

For seven agonizing days, the remaining members of the caravan labored through the pass. Some of the men's fingers and toes turned black with frostbite. Finally, they emerged from the icy pass. Although relieved to have made it through, each thought of the ones who hadn't. Twelve men had died and many of the oxen and horses. It was the most devastating loss Xuanzang would suffer on his journey, and those deaths weighed on his conscience.

The Great Khan

On the far side of the mountains, the winter-weary party was finally able to rest by the brackish, blue-black water of Lake Issyk Kul. After several days, the caravan slowly skirted the marshy lakeside before crossing a river and reaching the town of Tokmak. Because of the excellent hunting in the area, Tokmak was the winter headquarters for the Great Khan of the Western Turks.

Khan Yeh-hu warmly welcomed Xuanzang and his party. The Great Khan wore a robe of green satin and was surrounded by 200 officers dressed in silk brocade. The officers, in turn, were flanked by troops dressed in rich furs and mounted on camels and horses. Xuanzang waited patiently while the captain who had come with him from Turfan presented the gifts and the letter of introduction. After

The Turks and the Chinese

In the middle of the sixth century, the Turkic tribes were united, and their empire stretched from the Yellow Sea (near South Korea) to the Ural Mountains (which run north and south through western Russia).

About 584, the empire was split into two kingdoms, or *khanganates*. Each khanganate had a leader, called a Great Khan. The Eastern Great Khan and the Western Great Khan fought often. The Chinese emperors (first Emperor Gaozu and then Emperor Taizong) took advantage of the fighting by pitting one Great Khan against the other.

The Eastern Great Khan tried several times to invade China, but he failed. His own people then rebelled against him. Emperor Taizong used the rebellion to launch his own attack from 629 to 630, just as Xuanzang was trying to leave China.

China was successful in conquering the Eastern Great Khan. The Great Khan of the Western Turks then decided it was safer to be on friendly terms with China. He was welcomed at the Chinese court and remained as leader of his kingdom.

reading it, the Great Khan invited the whole party to a lavish banquet in his sumptuous yurt, a circular tent covered in felt.

The ruler called for music and wine and requested grape juice for Xuanzang, who did not drink alcohol. Steaming platters of boiled mutton and veal were heaped in front of the guests and the host, while Xuanzang gratefully received rice cakes, cream, sugar candy, raisins, and other fruit. Servants continually refilled everybody's cups. The men's laughter mingled with the unusual music played on many different instruments. The warmth, wine, and good food did much to improve everyone's mood.

Within days, the Great Khan, like other rulers Xuanzang met, was urging Xuanzang to stay. The monk refused politely: "I ask only that my party rest here for another few days," he said.

To Xuanzang's relief, the Great Khan did not protest further. Instead, he spent those days locating a man who knew Chinese as well as many other languages. "You must write letters of introduction from me," he commanded, "and accompany my friend." When Xuanzang's caravan was again ready to move on, the Great Khan gave him red satin robes and lengths of silk. As another mark of honor, the Khan and his officers accompanied the caravan for 5 kilometers (3 miles).

The next part of the journey was relatively easy, following a route that had been trampled smooth by thousands of feet and hooves. Sometimes the travelers stayed at monasteries, and, in the trade center of Che-shih, they enjoyed the luxury of a well-stocked *caravanserai*, with comfortable rooms for them and stalls for the animals.

Xuanzang and his group soon left for the ancient city of Samarkand in Sogdiana, a city grown rich from many centuries of Silk Road trade. At first, the countryside was well watered and fertile, with

Caravanserais

Prosperous merchants from Sogdiana often banded together to create permanent camps, or *caravanserais*, for their caravans at major trading centers along the Silk Road. Within these fancy caravanserais—the luxury hotels of the time—privileged travelers enjoyed the comforts of home and security for their beasts and drivers and for the treasures they transported. Poor travelers had to take their chances; sometimes the facilities were good, sometimes not.

A typical caravanserai had strong walls around it and one entrance wide enough for a loaded pack animal and cart. Inside, rooms backed onto the caravanserai walls. Each room had space for a merchant and his servants and goods. Some caravanserais also had stables or stalls for the animals; in others, the animals and their keepers stayed in an open central courtyard. At any time, yaks, camels, horses, oxen, and even elephants could be drinking from the same stone troughs.

In the caravanserai bazaars, merchants could sell goods or buy them, stocking up for the next leg of the trip. If they needed to exchange camels for yaks, or whatever animal was best for the terrain, they could do that too. Camels were ideal for sandy deserts; yaks were better in mountain country. The animal rental business worked well for the operators, the travelers, and the animals; owners got a decent trade-in price only if the animals were in good enough condition to serve a traveler headed back the other way.

towns dotted everywhere. But the travelers soon reached the last desolate region they would have to endure: the Desert of Red Sands, or Kizilkum, stretching ahead for 250 kilometers (155 miles).

The Red Sands

Kizilkum takes its name from the Turkic words *kizil*, meaning "red," and *kum*, meaning "sands." It is one of the largest deserts in the world, covering almost 300,000 square kilometers (116,00 square miles). Today, the desert is known for its deposits of gold, uranium, copper, aluminum, silver, natural gas, and oil.

Getting to Samarkand

Xuanzang now had experience traveling in the desert, and his party faithfully followed him into the wasteland. Once again, he saw his path disappear in the windblown sands, but this time he was not alone and he was not frightened.

His party, however, grew anxious. They had been traveling for days, with only a distant mountain to keep them on course. The bleached bones that littered the route were an ominous reminder that others had passed this way and had not made it out alive. But Xuanzang's calmness and unfailing belief that he was headed in the right direction helped to reassure them.

The sand was fine and deep, and sometimes their progress was slow. Xuanzang made sure that they rested frequently and were careful with their water. When the king of Turfan's soldiers had traveled with him, they had taught the monk a trick to use when he next crossed a desert: he carried a small stone and put it in his mouth when it was dry. It made his thirst tolerable and saved the water for those whom he was leading. Finally, his caravan emerged from Kizilkum. Not a single person had been lost in the desert crossing to Samarkand.

Samarkand was enormous, peopled by a blend of Sogdians and folk from many foreign lands. It was a city of palaces and gardens, wide paved avenues lined with trees, and warehouses bulging with expensive goods. It was also an industrial city, with a vast ironworks

Samarkand Stronghold

Like all Sogdian cities, Samarkand was built on a hill and heavily fortified with 15-meter-high (50-foot-high) walls and many towers from which defenders could repel an attack. In Xuanzang's time, the king was strong and his troops well trained.

that constantly belched black smoke. Xuanzang saw caravans carrying gems, spices, and cotton from India and others with silks and ironware from China bound for Persia and Rome. Bearded nomads from the north brought fur and hides to trade. Hundreds of caravanserais in the city found room for them all.

Everywhere in Samarkand, noise assaulted Xuanzang's ears. Merchants shouted out their wares, wagons creaked by, and the bells around camels' necks jingled. In the crowd, he bumped into a girl bargaining for onions, lamb, and spices for a stew. The aromas of food mingled with the smell of human sweat and animal dung made his nose wrinkle. He saw several of his party join a crowd cheering on a line of dancers. The women's embroidered skirts flared out above their light silk trousers as they whirled.

The Sogdian merchants that Xuanzang saw wore conical hats with the top turned forward, knee-long belted overjackets of silk brocade in rich colors, and narrow trousers tucked into brocade boots with leather soles.

Samarkand's king was at first disdainful of this foreign Buddhist monk. Without a monastery to use, Xuanzang preached in the markets. He had a powerful voice and always spoke clearly so that it was easy for his listeners to hear and understand. He soon drew large crowds each time he spoke.

Samarkand, Beloved of Poets

Over the centuries, the music of the name *Samarkand* has appealed to English poets who never saw the place, Milton and Keats among them. James Flecker wrote "The Golden Journey to Samarkand." He was a minor poet, but he is remembered for this one piece.

One very famous poet, however, lived in Samarkand for most of his adult life, moving there in 1070, long after Xuanzang's time. This was Omar Khayyam, author of *The Rubaiyat*, made famous in English poetry by Edward FitzGerald's translation.

Eventually, the king was so impressed that he allowed Xuanzang to call a congregation together and to ordain other Buddhist monks. This was remarkable because Buddhism was not recognized in Samarkand. No one worshipped at either of the two local temples; in fact, local inhabitants attacked anyone who tried to enter them. Xuanzang's powerful charisma had touched something deep in the king.

South to India

After a short stay in Samarkand, Xuanzang and his party made their first turn south, toward India. The Silk Road ran south and east through several small kingdoms and a spur of the high Pamir Mountains. After several days, they reached a narrow pass known as the Iron Gates, shut in on both sides by rust-colored mountain walls, which marked the boundary of the empire of the Western Turks. It was protected by double wooden doors, reinforced with iron, which could be closed in dangerous times. Because the Great Khan was not at war, the gates were open and Xuanzang and his caravan were able to continue southward.

After a brief stay at Kunduz, the caravan set out through the Snowy Mountains to Bamiyan. Pearls, gems, cotton, ivory, and spices from Sri Lanka passed through Bamiyan, moving along the Silk Road.

The Snowy Mountains

About the dangers of the Snowy Mountains, Xuanzang wrote vividly of "peaks and precipices fraught with peril. Wind and snow alternate incessantly, and at midsummer it is still cold. . . . The mountain tracks are hard to follow . . . and mountains are infested by troops of robbers who make murder their occupation."

After Xuanzang's party descended from the mountains and shook the last of the snow and ice from their furs, they saw something that stole their breath and brought the entire caravan to a standstill. Carved into niches in the towering sandstone cliffs, brightly colored and decorated with jewels, were two colossal Buddha statues. Their gilded hands and faces gleamed in the sun, the reflection almost blinding the travelers.

The Buddhas of Bamiyan

Xuanzang wrote the first description of the Buddha statues of Bamiyan, which were once the tallest standing Buddhas in the world. The statues were carved directly from the sandstone cliffs during the sixth century. Originally, they were covered with mud mixed with straw and then painted: the smaller Buddha statue, standing 37 meters (121 feet) tall, wore blue, while the larger one, at 55 meters (180 feet) high, wore red.

The world was shocked when the Taliban government of Afghanistan destroyed the Buddha statues in 2001. The great statues did not go easily; even with mortars, dynamite, tanks, anti-aircraft weapons, and rockets, it took three days to reduce them to piles of rubble and plaster. In 2003, the surrounding valley was designated by the United Nations Educational, Scientific and Cultural Organization (UNESCO) as a World Heritage Site. These are sites of cultural or natural importance for the world. The director-general of UNESCO called the demolition a crime against culture and a loss to humanity.

Why destroy the Buddhas? Taliban leaders said the statues insulted Islam, though most Muslim leaders in other countries disagreed.

Ancient Coins

Kapisa minted its own gold, silver, and copper coins. A coin found by archeologists centuries later shows an unknown king wearing a winged buffalo crown; on the reverse is a fire altar flanked by attendants, indicating that these people were Zoroastrians, worshippers of fire.

These bronze coins are the kind that Xuanzang might have used.

The Buddhas stood about a kilometer (a half-mile) apart with the biggest monastery in Bamiyan nestled between them. The monks' cells, as well as hundreds of chapels, were also carved from the pastel-colored sandstone cliffs and brightly painted with wonderful frescoes. Xuanzang wished they had more time to spend in the Bamiyan Valley; he wanted to know how the carvers had accomplished such an amazing feat. But India beckoned and the caravan lumbered on.

From Bamiyan, Xuanzang's caravan followed the Silk Road east, climbing to another dizzying pass in the Black Mountains. They emerged in the Ghorband River Valley, which led to Kapisa. It was the spring of 630, and the rainy season was coming. The caravan stopped in the capital, Kapisi, which had long been a major trade center on the Silk Road.

In the market, Xuanzang touched the delicately carved ivories from India, Chinese lacquerware, and Roman bronzes. He couldn't stop staring at an amazing glass vase depicting the Lighthouse of Alexandria, one of the seven wonders of the world.

When the rains began, Xuanzang took his rain-rest at a monastery before heading southeast toward Jalalabad. On the way, Xuanzang and his party passed fields of waving wheat, corn, and barley ready for the scythes; gradually these gave way to rice. Xuanzang was about to enter India.

Kapisa's Treasures

At Kapisa, many centuries later, archeologists excavated some of those Indian ivories, the Chinese lacquerware, all types of Roman bronzes, the glass vase, and many more treasures. Tragically, they were all lost when the Kabul museum was bombed during Afghanistan's civil war.

This Indian ivory carving dates from the second century and was found in 1939 in Afghanistan.

Reaching India

India was a wonder to Xuanzang. He was so eager to see everything in the land where Buddha was born that he barely slept. The yards of fabric in the colorful saris worn by the women and the long dhotis worn by the men intrigued him. He spent hours in the Buddhist monasteries, so different from those he was used to: these had a tower in each corner, tiered halls, and elaborate carvings on the wooden beams. The walls and doors were decorated, often in many colors. He was astounded by the number of religions in India, and the different sects within each, though he was dismayed by the squabbling that went on among them. Every night, squinting by the light of a whale oil candle, he wrote about the country and its people. He didn't want to forget anything.

Jalalabad was about 3500 kilometers (2175 miles) from Chang'an. Xuanzang had gone much farther, though, considering detours and winding roads. Now that he was in India, Xuanzang preferred to travel in easy stages on the trade routes of the Silk Road, since these were also the main thoroughfares. When Xuanzang was not on the move, he lived simply, giving his escorts a holiday or sending them home. Because of the letters of introduction he had, it was never difficult for Xuanzang to find guides or troops if he needed them. Important people everywhere wanted to meet him.

Xuanzang's India

Xuanzang divided his notes about India into 18 headings, including geographical extent and climate; measures of space and time; astronomy and the calendar; towns and buildings; commercial transactions; medicines and funeral customs; manners and administration of law; plants and trees; and food and drink. He wrote a summary under each.

Under "Towns and Buildings" he wrote, "As the ground is soft and muddy, the walls around towns and villages are mostly built of brick, with guard towers of wood or bamboo. The walls are wide and high; inside, however, the streets and lanes are narrow, tortuous and dirty. Main roads and lanes alike are crowded with stores and open stalls. Butchers, fishers, public entertainers, executioners and scavengers are compelled to live outside the walls and sneak along the left side of the road as they come and go. . . . Houses have wooden balconies coated with lime or mortar, and flat tiled roofs. These homes are higher than Chinese houses, but similar in structure. Walls are covered with lime and mud; floors are purified [*sic*] with cow's dung and strewn with flowers."

Northern India had recently been united under a strong and humane ruler, King Harsha. Xuanzang saw evidence of a settled and prosperous realm everywhere he went. The king was absent when Xuanzang first visited Kanyakubja, the capital, on the Ganges River, so the monk spent some time collecting flower and grain seeds.

As he traveled in India, Xuanzang paused frequently, stopping at monasteries for months at a time. At each monastery, he studied and had copies made of the scriptures kept there. When he could, he bought scriptures from the markets and had them checked against the originals. He also bought Buddha figures and commissioned replicas of those in the monasteries to be made in gold, silver, or sandalwood. He even collected relics of Buddha himself, such as fragments of his clothing.

In 637, Xuanzang reached Nalanda, a huge monastery and university. It was, at that time, the intellectual center of India. Xuanzang met monks from all over Asia who had followed Silk Road routes to reach Nalanda. They attended lectures on grammar, logic, Buddhist philosophy, Sanskrit, medicine, mathematics, astronomy, literature, and works of magic. Two hundred townspeople arrived at the monastery every day with hundreds of pounds of rice, butter, and milk. The monks' every need was met, including those for clothes, bedding, and medicines.

The day was divided into periods of study and worship, with water clocks keeping track of time. Xuanzang found experts to round out his knowledge of Sanskrit. Even better, he found a teacher: the master of Nalanda, the Venerable Shilabhadra.

When he met Xuanzang, tears poured down the teacher's cheeks. "You have come at last," he whispered. "You have come!" The teacher explained that arthritis had ravaged his joints for the past 20 years. Sometimes life didn't seem worth living. But he knew that

Water Clocks

Many types of water clocks were used in Xuanzang's time. The water clock at Nalanda was made of two bowls: a large bowl filled with water and a smaller copper bowl with two floats resting in it, markings along its inside walls to indicate hours, and a tiny hole in its bottom. When the copper bowl was placed in the water-filled bowl, the water would steadily leak through the hole, carrying the floats upward with the rising water level. When the floats reached a new marking, it meant another hour had passed. Students watched over the clocks and rang a gong to signal each hour.

A modern example of the water clocks Xuanzang saw at Nalanda

a monk would come someday from China. He would teach this monk everything he knew, and the pleasure of teaching would make his pain bearable.

Xuanzang studied at Nalanda for three years. The students there, overseen by Xuanzang, carefully made copies in Sanskrit of many scriptures and Buddhist writings. Those at Nalanda were pleased to help spread the word of Buddhism to China. Buddhism was declining in India, and the Hindu religion was gaining importance. Xuanzang went back to Nalanda twice after exploring other parts of India.

The Peaceful King

Xuanzang met King Harsha late in his journey, in 642. This unusual ruler wrote poetry and plays; some of his work is still performed on stages today. King Harsha worshiped the sun, but he also respected India's other great religions: Hinduism and Buddhism. During his years in India, Xuanzang studied other religions and every variation within his own.

Xuanzang had questioned his religious beliefs all his life, needing to learn more and reconsider things whenever he added to his knowledge. At King Harsha's court, Xuanzang often debated with religious leaders of other faiths, as much to test himself as to convince others.

King Harsha found these exchanges fascinating, and he often turned the debates into events. The king's people would serve platters of fruit and baskets of cheese while the men spoke. King Harsha was very impressed by the breadth of Xuanzang's religious understanding. Other people, however, were not happy about the monarch's fondness for the Buddhist monk.

Before Xuanzang's arrival, King Harsha had been careful to balance the competing religions in his kingdom by appointing officials from each one. Now, though, he began to favor Buddhists over Hindus and sun worshippers, which made many people angry. Some

About a year later, his party had to cross the Indus River, near the city of Hund. It was a massive undertaking to get everyone and everything in the boats. Throughout the preparations, Xuanzang anxiously kept an eye on the skies as they began to darken. They were in the middle of the crossing when his fears were realized: the storm hit hard and a wave almost swamped one of the boats.

Xuanzang watched helplessly as 50 of his precious books went overboard, along with all the seeds he had collected. The monk felt his heart sink with them into the murky water. He slowly shook his head as the rain pelted him, reminding himself that none of his party had been drowned. He thanked Buddha for his mercy. "We have lost a few goods," Xuanzang told the group, "but they can be replaced. Life is the greatest treasure we own."

Xuanzang had made careful notes of where he had collected each book and who had made the copies. He was still determined to take a complete collection of Buddhist sacred writings home to China, so he sent people back for copies of the missing books.

Xuanzang waited in Hund as patiently as he could. After almost two months with no word of the books, the caravan went on and began to climb the Hindu Kush Mountains.

Wild precipices alternated with caverns and hollows as the party ascended. Although it was July in 644, frozen drifts still blocked the peaks; the troops had to cut steps in the ice for the group as they climbed. The elephant struggled with the frozen staircase, but its bulk made a good windbreak, and they often used the elephant to open a path in the snow for the horses and carts to follow.

Most of the extra porters they had hired in Hund gave up the grueling journey long before the summit and returned home. The descent took three days, but finally Xuanzang spotted a few huts and some small monasteries. After resting for five days, the travelers pushed on to Kunduz. There, Xuanzang waited, once again, for his missing books. After a month, still without the books, the caravan journeyed on through the Pamir Mountains.

At Tashkurgan, the first small oasis kingdom on the far side of the mountains, a group of merchants approached Xuanzang and asked to join the caravan. The monk agreed. Five days later, another band of robbers on the Silk Road ambushed the party. Instead of attacking directly, these fearsome horsemen rode around Xuanzang's group in two large circles going in opposite directions, kicking up dust and causing the horses in Xuanzang's caravan to wheel around in confusion.

Xuanzang kept a tight grip on his reins and called for the others to do the same. The dust choked him as the

Elephants were often used in warfare in India. This painting dates from the 14th century.

bandits began driving the whole caravan forward. When anyone tried to break through, a swirling sword would cut the air in front of him or an arrow would whizz past his ear.

Unexpectedly, the group of merchants made a break for it, and the other horses in the caravan followed them, sides heaving with fear. Their riders could barely stay on and couldn't turn their mounts. The thieves, on sure-footed hill ponies, galloped after them, driving them into a tight ravine. King Harsha's terrified elephant found itself trapped in the narrow gorge and suddenly stampeded. Men and animals scrambled to get out of its way. In blind fear, the elephant trampled several of the thieves, whose screams caused the rest to turn their ponies and flee.

Now seeing a way out of the gorge, the mighty beast charged. Xuanzang desperately tried to cut across the elephant's path and turn the animal, but it was maddened by panic. At the last second, Xuanzang had to yank his horse sharply to the side as the elephant thundered past, toppled into the river, and drowned.

Buddhists treat the lives of animals and humans with equal respect, and Xuanzang squeezed his eyes shut as he said a prayer for the mighty elephant. They might not have survived the snowy mountain pass without it, and its actions here had likely saved their lives again. It was a downhearted company that tramped through the sand dunes on the road to Khotan.

The markets along the Silk Road still sell their wonderful melons, though not the same varieties as those Xuanzang ate.

As sand gave way to irrigated land, the smell of sweet fruit filled Xuanzang's nostrils. In the orchards, he watched farmers pick late-ripening apricots, figs, apples, pomegranates, and pistachios. Fields of fat melons waited to be harvested.

Khotan was the biggest and most prosperous oasis on the Silk Road. Under clear September skies, the king of Khotan rode out to meet his guest, partly because he hoped to foster closer ties with China.

Xuanzang stayed in one of Khotan's many monasteries. Still determined to take home a complete collection of Buddhist scriptures, he decided to remain until his copies caught up with him. He sent home King Harsha's men and the others who had traveled with him from India. While Xuanzang waited, he wrote a letter to Emperor

How Distance Was Measured in China and India

I n China, a *li* is a measure of length. In Xuanzang's time, one *li* was approximately 325 meters (1065 feet). The modern *li* has been standardized at 500 meters (1640 feet). Two *li* equal 1 kilometer (about half a mile).

In his book, Xuanzang described the units of distance used in India. The *yojana* (pronounced yu-shen-na) was how far an army could march in one day. Trying to convert *li* to *yojana*, Xuanzang used three sources, all different: 1 *yojana* might be 40 *li*, 30 *li*, or only 16 *li*. Today, 1 *yojana* equals 8 *kroshas* (pronounced keu-ru-she): a *krosha* is the distance that a cow's mooing can be heard.

Taizong. "I accomplished a journey of more than fifty thousand *li*." Xuanzang's hand shook a little; he had disobeyed the emperor's orders when he had left China 16 years before. "I have won for my emperor the high esteem and praise of the people."

Xuanzang was returning from India with 520 cases of books, Buddha statues, and relics. Would the emperor welcome him? It was possible that the emperor would take the treasures but not allow Xuanzang to translate the books.

When the reply came, Xuanzang opened it nervously, but Emperor Taizong was not angry. The emperor was well aware that the Buddhist monk had been his unofficial goodwill ambassador abroad. He wrote, "I am highly delighted to hear that the teacher is returning home after seeking the Way in foreign lands. You may come to see me as quickly as possible."

Xuanzang let his breath out in a rush of relief. He was going home and would be welcomed.

Home at Last in China

A few months later, the missing books finally arrived, and Xuanzang set out immediately. Emperor Taizong sent carriers to transport everything to Chang'an.

Taizong himself could not be at Chang'an when Xuanzang arrived, but he sent a high official instead. Xuanzang's eyes widened as he saw the city's residents leave their work and homes and crowd into the main streets to celebrate his return. Hundreds of monks wearing ceremonial robes helped parade the precious books and relics from the Street of the Red Bird to the Monastery of Great Happiness. It was the most splendid event since the death of the Buddha. Xuanzang's heart was filled with pride.

Emperor Taizong was at Luoyang, and Xuanzang lost no time in going to meet him. The emperor's first question was direct. "Why did you go to India without telling me?"

Xuanzang apologized. "I had sent several petitions, but I did not receive the favor of an official permission. Because of my sincerity in seeking the Law, I went away privately, for which offence I beg pardon of Your Majesty."

"You are a monk," shrugged the emperor. "You are different from those outside the clergy. No need for you to ask my pardon."

Both the emperor and the monk had changed over the years. Xuanzang had crossed forbidding lands. He had dealt with soldiers, faced down robbers, lived with kings, and met people whose cultures, values, beliefs, and appearance were very different from his own. He was poised and confident, no longer the hothead who had defied the king of Turfan.

The Great Wild Goose Pagoda was the library the emperor built to hold Xuanzang's treasures. Though it has changed since Xuanzang's time, it still stands in Xi'an today, and is a popular tourist attraction.

Taizong was now the secure ruler of China and ready to expand his diplomatic connections. For hours, he questioned Xuanzang about the Western countries: places, people, climate, goods, stories, music, and art. "You must write a book for me," he said at last. "Nobody else has seen as much as you. This is the most important thing you can do for the people of China."

Xuanzang did not agree. Translating his collection of Buddhist books from Sanskrit into Chinese was more important to him. But the emperor raised his chin and looked down at Xuanzang. "If you choose not to write the book for me, then I cannot help with your translations. You will have to find your own way." Xuanzang felt butterflies in his stomach. "But if you first write the book for me, I will allow you to design a building for your books," he said. "You can then name the monks who will live there and help you to translate the Buddha's words. You will never lack for food and servants."

Xuanzang knew when he was beaten. "Your majesty is very generous," he said diplomatically. "Of course I will write your book."

For more than a year, Xuanzang wrote some sections of the book and dictated others. He had made many detailed entries in his logs, and his memory was extraordinary. The emperor sent him an experienced editor, a monk named Bianchi. The men worked well together. They crafted the book by using a writing brush, fine paper that would later be glued together to form scrolls, an ink stick, and an ink stone against which the stick was rubbed to produce lustrous black ink.

After his book was completed in 646, Xuanzang worked long days translating the religious texts he had collected and talking to Emperor Taizong about his beliefs. Before the emperor died, he became a Buddhist. The new emperor, Gaozong, continued to support Xuanzang's work.

The Great Wild Goose Pagoda

The Great Wild Goose Pagoda is the library in which Xuanzang translated so many of the precious books. The library is now a tourist attraction in Xi'an, the modern city built on the ruins of ancient Chang'an. In the grounds of the monastery next door, elaborate shrines commemorate Buddhist leaders. One small shrine shows only a Chinese monk's name. Why was this monk so special?

During the Cultural Revolution in China (1966 to 1976), Chairman Mao did not believe that reading and study were useful, so nobody brought food to the monasteries. The monks had to leave or starve. But the last monk at the Great Wild Goose Pagoda did not leave. Somehow, he kept himself alive. Because of this one man, the monastery survived; now it is home to monks who care for the library and guide visitors. He was, indeed, special.

Shortly after it was built in the mid-seventh century, the Great Wild Goose Pagoda collapsed, only to be rebuilt and have five extra stories added. In 1556, an earthquake destroyed three levels, and it has stood at seven stories ever since.

Two Books

Xuanzang's book, called *Records of the Western World*, was completed in 646. This book has enlightened historians, archeologists, and other scholars ever since. In fact, it is the only source for huge chunks of the history and geography of Xuanzang's time. It was through another book, *The Life of Hiuen-Tsiang*—using a different spelling than we have for the monk's name—that the world learned about Xuanzang himself. The admiring biography was written by Hwui Li, one of the monks assigned to work on the Buddhist translations with Xuanzang. Xuanzang's notes described his personal journey, but he did not include them in his book for the emperor. He appears to have told his disciples about his adventures, and the stories likely circulated throughout the monastery. Hwui Li, who wrote the biography between 664 and 688, brought the traveling monk to life and made him an enduring hero of Chinese folklore.

It took Xuanzang and the 23 monks who worked with him 19 years to translate into Chinese all the books that he had brought back. He was an exacting taskmaster; sometimes whole translations had to be redone when they didn't meet his expectations. He also dealt with countless interruptions along the way. He was always in demand to teach and to translate official messages written in Sanskrit and other works sent by the kings he had met.

Needing to reconnect with his spiritual side, Xuanzang had moved to a monastery outside Chang'an in 651 while continuing his translation work. Then, in 664, he could feel his death approaching. He spent time meditating and saying goodbye to the Buddha statues he had commissioned. He gave away his few belongings and said his farewells to monks of the monastery, his disciples, and his translators. Finally, he lay in bed, his breathing slowed, and he died peacefully. More than 1 million people attended his funeral.

Xuanzang died with the deep satisfaction of knowing that he had carried out his spiritual mission: the scriptures he brought back to China helped to transform the religion of his country. But during his mission, he had achieved other things. He had preserved a priceless, unique record of all the lands through which he passed. Precious gems, spices, horses, silk, ivory, religion, and so much more traveled the Silk Road in the seventh century—without Xuanzang, the world might never have known.

How Accurate Was Xuanzang?

Much of Xuanzang's *Records of the Western World* can't be verified. Scholars check what they can, however, and they continue to be impressed by Xuanzang's accuracy. Early in the 20th century, British explorer Sir Aurel Stein used Xuanzang's ancient measurements and his descriptions of the cities, mountains, and rivers along the route to locate many oasis ruins. Because we know he was right about so many details, we have good reason to believe Xuanzang was right about ones that can't be checked.

Xuanzang's estimates were not perfect. Sometimes he gave a range: a journey of 1400 or 1500 *li* over a mountain and into a valley brought him to Nepal. His description of each new kingdom began with its circumference: Nepal was "above 4000 *li* in circuit"; its capital was "above 20 *li* in circuit."

Where did these numbers come from? Almost certainly Xuanzang could judge distances on land with great accuracy. He augmented his keen observations with local records and whatever other information he could gather, and put it all together.

GENGHIS KHAN

Spread of the Mongol empire

CHAPTER 2

The Silk Road and the Warrior: Genghis Khan

The Silk Road

In some ways, the Silk Road itself did not change between Xuanzang's return to China in 645 and Genghis Khan's birth in 1162. The journeys remained long and difficult, and unlucky travelers still got lost in desert sandstorms or buried by mountain avalanches. But the borders of countries shifted many times. Some of the countries the Silk Road ran through united and became powerful, and others lost power and were conquered. Northern India broke into small feuding kingdoms when King Harsha died in 647.

Early in the eighth century, Tibet became strong. Its ruler conquered the oasis kingdoms and cut off trade between Sogdiana and China. Within China, rebellion weakened the Tang Dynasty and made China vulnerable to attack. China had once fought with the Uighurs, but the Chinese asked their former enemies for help. The Uighurs took over the oasis kingdoms and threw out the Tibetan soldiers. But the price for their help was high. The Uighurs made China agree to buy horses from them at a price of forty bolts of silk for each horse. Over the years, the Uighurs sold thousands of horses to China. The bills got higher and higher. Finally, China owed more for the horses than the value of all the silk in the country. When the Tang emperor tried to send back some horses, the Uighurs threatened to allow other nomads to invade China. The Tang Dynasty lost power, and its rule ended in 906. Not until 961 was China reunited under the Song Dynasty.

In Mongolia, many different clans or groups lived, only one of which was the Mongols. Around 1130, the Mongols became a strong force and conquered other clans, only to lose power again just before Genghis Khan was born.

Genghis Khan sat perfectly still atop his battle-hardened Mongolian horse. The heavy-boned animal shook its big head and pawed the ground, seemingly eager for what was to come. The Great Khan was about to launch his most ambitious attack so far.

Before the Khan lay the state of Western Xia, the home of the Tanguts, a nomadic clan with ties to China. It had a huge network of fortified cities, with an army of 150,000 men, and was home to almost 5 million people. The Silk Road wove its way through the kingdom, and bringing Western Xia under his control meant Genghis Khan would control more of this valuable trading route. He needed the Silk Road routes so that his invading armies could move more rapidly.

Dating from the 14th century, this painting shows the Mongols charging fearlessly into battle.

Behind him, his men waited for his signal. They had followed him across almost 1000 kilometers (620 miles) of empty plains to get here, but they looked much the same as when they had first set out. Most of the ferocious warriors were short and stocky, like their horses. Their leathery skin shone with the grease they used to protect it. Having lived their whole lives on the move, looking after herds of animals on the barren steppes of Asia, they were used to harsh conditions.

The sun glinted off their brass and iron helmets, their leather neck protectors hanging down in back. Unlike most armies, the Mongol soldiers wore light armor. Over their fur-lined coats and raw silk shirts were just four overlapping plates made hard with lacquer. Most soldiers used bows and arrows as weapons. These men could shoot an arrow more than 200 meters (655 feet) with deadly accuracy. A few also carried sabers and maces. Some carried long hooked staffs made to yank a man from his horse in battle.

Giving Signals

Genghis Khan had worked out a system of hand signals to direct his troops. As a result, the Khan could move his men quickly and easily in battle. Sometimes, when hand signals would be hard to see, generals controlled battle movements with black and white flags, banners, or smoke signals during the day, and torches at night. Although they often used drums and war cries, Mongol troops could move and fight in silence if they had to. To their enemies, it seemed as if they moved together by magic or with guidance from an unseen hand. The eerie silence sometimes caused enemies to panic and flee.

Silk as Armor

The raw silk shirts worn by the Mongol warriors were nothing like the fine, delicate fabric that shirts are made from today. Raw silk is tough, and it has thick and thin strands woven together, giving it a rough surface. The silk could save a warrior's life if he was hit by an arrow. As the arrow bit into the skin, the silk would neatly fold itself around the arrowhead and stay intact. Removing the arrow was then made easier by pulling on the cloth to release the arrowhead. Sometimes, the silk even kept the poison painted on arrowheads from spreading into the bloodstream.

The Story of Silk

Silk Trade Secrets

As early as 3000 BCE, people in China had discovered the way to raise silkworms and make silk, called sericulture. China closely guarded its secret. For hundreds of years, anyone trying to leave China with silkworms or cocoons was arrested and killed. How did the secret finally leak out? The most popular story says that a Chinese princess was to marry a foreign prince, perhaps from India, more likely from nearby Khotan. The bride hid silkworm eggs and mulberry seeds in her elaborate headdress when she traveled to her new country. Because she was a princess, nobody searched her when she crossed the Chinese border. She got away with her smuggling. Chinese silk was still the best, but by 300 CE, Korea, India, and Japan were also producing silk. The Roman Empire, Spain, and Sicily soon followed, with the method slowly spreading to the rest of Europe.

In this scene, painted on a vase from the Ming Dynasty, a family weaves threads into silk.

The Life of a Silkworm

Silkworms are the caterpillars of a fat moth called *Bombyx mori*. They have been bred over 5000 years to have such tiny wings that they cannot fly. *Bombyx* caterpillars can eat only mulberry leaves.

In Xuanzang's time, for six months of every year, silk was the main business of many Chinese families. Women hatched eggs from silkworm moths and raised

A woman carefully picks leaves from a mulberry tree in this 19th-century painting.

them at home. The silkworms needed constant attention. Their mulberry leaves had to be chopped fine for the first few days. The silkworms ate a lot, gaining 10,000 times their birth weight within a month! The silkworms then spun puffy white balls for their cocoons. Sadly, the only way to harvest the silk was to kill the silkworms. The women baked or steamed the cocoons. (People then ate the worms. They were an excellent source of protein, even richer than beef.)

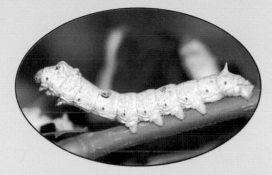

A silkworm crawls along a mulberry branch.

Silkworm farmers dipped the cocoons in hot water to loosen the fiber so they could unwind it. One cocoon yielded a thin strand, very strong and light, that was anywhere from five hundred or six hundred meters up to two kilometers (just over a mile) long. Five to eight strands were twisted together to form a thread that could be spun, dyed, and woven into cloth. It took 25,000 cocoons to make one pound (half a kilogram) of silk!

Making Silk Today

China still produces about 70 percent of the world's silk. India makes about 12 percent, with most of the rest coming from Japan, Russia, Vietnam, and Brazil. Many kinds of mulberry trees and bushes have been developed to suit different climates and feed the silkworms.

More than 95 percent of all silk still comes from silk moths that people raise. Silk produced by *Bombyx* caterpillars is white, fine, and even. Some wild moths, especially in India, make small amounts of special silk yarn. Wild caterpillars eat many kinds of leaves, which makes their cocoons different colors, including cream, stone, honey, and dark brown. Wild yarn tends to be thicker, producing a heavy, textured fabric. Today, anyone can raise silkworms. You can order silkworms and prepared silkworm food, if you don't have mulberry trees. Be warned—raising silkworms is very hard.

A silkworm cocoon

Genghis Khan's army units included each soldier's household and animals. They, and their houses, often moved all together.

Genghis believed that his army was ready. When he became the Great Khan, he had devised a new system for his soldiers. He reorganized them into military units of 10, 100, 1000, and 10,000 warriors, together with the men's households and animals. By mingling men from different clans in the units of 10, he made it impossible for one clan to fight another. By making a unit commander responsible for his men, he let each soldier know that he was valued. Mongolia had a small population, perhaps 2 million people at most. Because Genghis had much smaller forces than his opponents did, each soldier *did* matter, militarily, at least. In return, his men were fiercely loyal to him.

When the Great Khan was ready, he gave the hand signal. As the small Mongolian horses leapt forward, war drums boomed in time with the pounding of their hooves. Each beat was meant to rattle the enemy, though the drums were soon drowned out by the blood-curdling war cries of the Mongol archers. With perfectly trained mounts that responded instantly to commands the bowmen gave with their legs and feet, the archers had their hands free. They fired arrow after arrow while moving at top speed, rarely missing a target and making themselves difficult to hit.

The Tangut troops were also seasoned fighters, though. They met every attempt with a solid defense, sometimes giving ground but often pushing the Mongol army back. Even with Genghis's careful planning, it was his first attack on a city. His troops were used to fighting on the open plains, where their fast-moving horses gave them an advantage. The Khan soon learned his cavalry couldn't win against an army fighting from a fortified place.

So Genghis did what he always did: he pretended to retreat to the foothills. His men seemed to disappear, except for a small group of stragglers that the Tangut generals could see. Immediately, the Tanguts gave chase, leaving their protected position and exposing their weaknesses. As soon as they reached the small group of Genghis's men, the rest of the Mongols poured back from the hills and ruthlessly cut down the large Tangut army. The Khan had won his first victory in Western Xia, but many more would be needed.

Genghis Khan's Story

The story of Genghis Khan and his family is told in a long epic poem called *The Secret History of the Mongols*. No one knows who wrote the poem, but it was likely created around the year 1240. No original written in Mongolian has ever been found. The oldest copies that have survived are from the 14th century and have Mongolian words spelled out in Chinese phonetic translations. Phonetic words are spelled exactly how they would sound when spoken. *The Secret History of the Mongols* is the one of the greatest poems ever written by wanderers like the Mongols, and it is the best record we have of life and events in Mongolia in the time of Genghis Khan.

The Early Years

He hadn't always been Genghis Khan, of course. When he was born on the northern steppes of Asia in 1162, his father, a Mongol clan chief, had named him Temujin. The Mongols lived in large groups called clans, and they made their living by caring for their herds of animals. Horses were their most prized animals, and the Mongols were well known as excellent riders. Children learned to ride at the same time as they learned to walk, and they spent much of their childhood on horseback. The Mongols also raised yaks, sheep, goats, camels, and, in the northwest, reindeer. Their herds gave them meat, hair, skins, dung for fuel, milk, and felt for clothing and for their portable homes.

The extreme climate of their homeland forced the Mongols to be tough, but they relied on their animals for survival. Any serious danger to their animals, such as heavy snows, droughts, or disease, also put their own lives in danger.

The Mongols lived in large groups on the barren steppes. They survived by caring for their herds of animals.

له انسوني برمي جواسد وسلمها ان اصلاح دراب مي هند وباردي بسيار نع سد ان ظرف ذرمه باني
ولوان مثنها بيون اين و درزموضعي كه آمرا كنيند فرومانند ومشهور درت كه درزان موضع بوروف
كريا او متيقن شند دست و باجان شهدت سرما طاشند ودمه قمارگي تاعاني بوده كه بسياري مردم و
وافلال شنه نجنيككرخان وادكخان نكبار اراك لسني حزيره مقام كرده بو

ودران وقت جابوته نيز ماجماعتي كه اورا لكي بركرانه بودند بامروق خان بهم آمده بودند حوز حال الر
جنيككرخان كردوخانه آن نوم كه اوبافشاهي بركردند عارت كرده كرده بخدمت جنيككرخان آمدو

Mongolian Food

When they were on the move, the Mongols ate wild vegetables and meat from the animals they herded and hunted. In spring and summer, they drank mare's or ewe's milk and made yogurt and cheese, setting the *aruul* (dried cheese curds) to dry on top of the ger. Mare's milk has four times as much vitamin C as cow's milk. In winter, the Mongols ate more meat. There weren't many trees on the grassy plains, so the Mongols used animal dung as cooking fuel. The children used baskets to collect the droppings.

Going It Alone

Temujin's life became much harder after his father died. Although he had a claim to the title of chief, his father's followers refused to be led by a boy. Upset by the leader's death, and needing to be in a strong clan to stay safe, they transferred their loyalty elsewhere, leaving Temujin's family on their own. Even Temujin's uncles, who should have helped the family, abandoned them, leaving them just two horses. On the unforgiving steppes, a family alone would need more horses to survive.

Huge herds of semi-wild horses roamed the grasslands. When a boy was 11 or 12 years old, he would catch his first horse and break it for riding. It was his major test in becoming a man. Temujin and his brothers would have to pass that test early.

When Temujin's turn came, he had already made a careful plan. He wouldn't try to overtake a wild herd while riding, the way his oldest brother, Begter, did. A frightened horse running alone could usually not be caught—and if it could, it wasn't much of a horse. Using a neck loop, or lasso, on a wild free-running horse could break its neck. But Begter was often impulsive and acted without thinking. He had been lucky to catch an old broken-down mare. Still the animal would be useful.

Temujin waited until spring to try. He knew the wild horses would be at their weakest after spending months rooting through snow to find grasses. He took his time, riding out early, watching the small bronze- and copper-colored beasts. Their shaggy winter coats hid just how thin they were. He found a herd whose territory included a watering hole near a blind gully. A blind gully is a narrow channel carved out by a river that has since dried up. Blind gullies end abruptly in a high wall.

On the day he was ready, Temujin approached his family's only stallion. He held the beast and carefully peeled the top layer from its chestnuts. The chestnuts are hard patches of skin that grow and shed continually on the inside of a horse's legs. Temujin then rubbed the stallion's skin on his hands, neck, hair, and clothes. This would help to hide his scent from the wild horses.

Then he hid himself in some brush, just behind the watering hole, and left his own horse close by as a lure. He knew the wild horses would approach his trap near the end of the day. Nervously, Temujin kept peeking out and strained to hear them. He needed his plan to work. As the sun slowly began to sink, his ears caught a faint nicker. They were coming! They tossed their heads and whinnied when they saw Temujin's horse, but the young mare posed no threat. Seeing the mare distracted them, though, and they walked right past Temujin. In his hiding place, he balled his hands into fists. He had to be patient and stay still; he had to wait until they had drunk their fill. A horse with a belly full of water could not run very fast or for long.

His whole body seemed to vibrate with tension. He squinted through the brush, trying to see the horses and choose the ones that

Mongolian Horses

Mongolian horses provided more than just transportation. People used their milk, meat, and blood for food, their hides to make leather, and their sinews for bowstrings and for sewing. Fermented mare's milk (called *kumiss* or *airag*) was the favorite Mongol drink. Horse tendons were boiled slowly for several days to make glue, which was used for everything from arrows to carts.

would be easiest to catch and would serve the family best. As the horses finished drinking and lifted their heads one by one, Temujin exploded from his hiding place behind them, a war cry escaping his throat to scare and scatter the herd.

It worked! The horses spooked as he grabbed his mare and vaulted onto her back. Hooves pounding the sandy soil, the wild creatures raced toward the blind valley, hoping to escape. Their long manes and tails streamed behind them, and Temujin let out a whoop as he chased them through the choking cloud of dust kicked up by their flying hooves.

Heavy with the water it had drunk, a young horse began to fall behind. There! That was the one Temujin would take. He pushed his mount up, closer to the young horse, nudging it toward the gully. Taking some comfort from Temujin's mare, the colt began to move away from the herd and into the gully.

Suddenly, the wall was right in front of them. Panicked, the young horse tried to turn, but Temujin's larger mount blocked its escape. Now Temujin could use his leather rope. The Mongolian horses' short, thick necks made it tough to throw a loop of rope from behind. So he worked his mare closer, using her hindquarters to keep the young animal near the side of the narrow gully, with the wall

in front. Slowly, carefully, he made a short throw to the side and over the horse's head. Success!

With his horse firmly caught, Temujin wasted no time running a rope from the one on its neck under its belly, tying it to the base of the animal's tail. This would keep the horse from raising its head. If it couldn't raise its head, it couldn't run, but it could still walk. When he stood up, Temujin's legs shook just a little. He gently touched the young horse's heaving flanks, and he could feel it trembling under his fingers. He murmured softly into its ear, trying to calm it—and himself—a little. His first horse! He had done it. He *was* worthy of leading a clan.

He slowly led the colt home behind his mare, removed the tying rope, and left the animal in a makeshift corral with some fodder. He had made the corral out of the same kind of poles and felt as his family's ger. It would give the captive time to adjust and give Temujin a place to break his new horse slowly and get him used to being ridden.

By the end of their first year, the family had a small herd of nine horses.

Whatever It Takes

Temujin, his mother, and his two brothers often went hungry, and sometimes they were in danger of starving to death. The family lived on what they could find or catch: fish, berries, wild onions, field mice, or small birds.

Begter often bullied the two younger boys. As the years wore on, he began taking the fish or the birds they caught and would not share. Each time, Temujin had to swallow the lump of anger in his throat. No matter what their mother did, Begter continued to steal their food. Finally, when Temujin was about 13, he truly felt that the rest of the family's survival was at stake. He would have to take drastic measures. He went to find his younger brother.

"We will have to kill Begter," he told him flatly.

The boy stared at Temujin in shock, and they spent hours debating the plan. Eventually, the younger boy ran out of arguments, hung his head, and nodded. They waited until their oldest brother was alone on the plain, guarding the horses.

Quietly, they crept up behind Begter, careful not to alert him. Temujin's hand on his bow was rock steady, while his younger brother's shook just a little. They each drew an arrow. Leaving his younger brother hidden, Temujin jumped out in front of Begter. The older boy was startled for a moment, and then his features settled into his characteristic sneer. "Am I supposed to be afraid of you and your bow, little brother?" He arched one eyebrow scornfully. "Leave me alone and find me something to eat." He waved his hand dismissively.

Temujin's face never changed as he nocked his arrow, raised the bow, and quickly let the arrow fly, straight into Begter's chest. At almost the same time, his younger brother, too, let his arrow go, hitting Begter in the back. As Begter fell, Temujin made no move to catch him. Instead, he stepped over him, picked up Begter's bow, and headed for the ger. Only when he was sure his younger brother could no longer see him did Temujin close his eyes tightly and clench his fists to stop them from trembling. It was done.

Building a Clan

The marriage of one chief's son to another chief's daughter was a common way to cement a friendship between two clans. Temujin's father had chosen his son's bride, Borte, when she was only 10 years old and Temujin was 9. Now, Temujin was 18, and he was ready to

called the Keraits. Toghril had been Temujin's father's ally. The ruler was impressed with Temujin. The young man was already known as a skilled horseman and raider. A few Mongol soldiers had even joined his clan, and now Temujin had married the daughter of a chief. Toghril agreed to provide protection in return for the gift of the valuable coat. Temujin had made his first crucial alliance.

Losing Borte and Becoming Khan

Years earlier, Temujin's father had stolen a bride from another clan called the Merkits. When the Merkits heard that Temujin was now married, they made a plan to raid his small encampment to capture the new bride and kill Temujin.

It was a clear, quiet morning just before dawn, and the couple had been married just less than a year. The small group had made camp in a broad valley with lush grass and water nearby. The herds that Temujin had gathered were grazing contentedly, and the clan members were still sleeping, except for one old woman who was stirring the fire to life. Suddenly, she felt the throbbing in the ground of hundreds of horses galloping into the valley.

"It's a raid! It's a raid! Temujin, wake up—you must escape," she shouted. "If they catch you, they will surely kill you." If the clan leader was killed, the rest of the group would be kept as slaves.

Temujin leapt from his ger, grabbed his horse, and swung himself up onto its back in one smooth move. The others in the camp soon did the same. The other men galloped away at once, but Temujin paused, looking down at Borte. He saw the fear in her face, but she knew the Merkits would kill him if they caught him.

"Go, husband," she implored. "I can hide myself and you can lead these raiders into the mountains, where they will be lost." Still her husband hesitated. "We will be together again soon. Go!"

Temujin could see the Merkits coming into the valley at the far end and knew he had little time left. "I will come back for you," he shouted as he kicked his horse hard and fled with the others.

Only the old woman, named Koagchin, and Borte were left, with one horse. Koagchin had survived many raids in her years, and she was already hitching the horse to a wagon loaded with wool. "Quickly— hide yourself under the wool. I will

pretend I was here just to help with sheep shearing." Borte jumped into the back of the cart and covered herself. The raiders were almost on them, and Koagchin urged the horse on. But the old cart could not handle the added weight of the woman in the back. When it hit a rut in the ground, an axle broke and a wheel flew off, causing Borte to tumble out.

The Merkits quickly captured both women. They soon realized from the way she was dressed that Borte was the clan chief's wife. They decided that taking her was revenge enough. Perhaps Temujin would even come to them, hoping to rescue her. They took their prize and headed back to their camp, some 300 kilometers (185 miles) to the north.

When Temujin and his group returned to camp hours later, they found it empty, except for the broken cart. He felt heat rise to his face and prickle his scalp as he realized what had happened. Temujin gathered his clan and immediately sent messengers to Toghril, his new ally, and to Jamuka, a neighboring chieftain and childhood friend, asking for help to rescue his young wife.

It took some time, but both leaders came to his aid, each with an army. Some 12,000 men were ready to go to war with the

Merkits and rescue Borte. Temujin was chosen to lead the combined forces because it was his wife at risk. When they were ready, he sat astride his horse and looked back at the men behind him, awaiting his command. It was his first experience as a general and he drank in the feeling of strength and power it offered. He and his troops headed out after the kidnappers.

The force that Temujin led was too large to use the element of surprise. So even though they arrived at night, a lookout saw them coming and warned the Merkits, who fled in all directions. Borte was terrified. She didn't know that her husband led this army or that they were there for her. All she could see were horsemen with sabers cutting down the men around her; all she could hear were screams as men died. She was grabbed by a Merkit and thrown into a cart.

"Borte!" Temujin shouted over the thundering of the hooves. "Borte! It's Temujin." He raced around the camp, calling his wife's name.

"I am here!" she shouted, jumping from the cart. She scrambled toward her husband, narrowly missing being trampled by the horses' sharp hooves. Temujin heard her voice, swung from his horse, and threw open his arms to grab her. He took her out of the camp while his men killed the wounded Merkits and captured others for slaves. Many had managed to flee. His men soon found Koagchin, and the rescue was complete.

After this victory, many clans came to join Temujin, and he became determined to unite the Mongol clans under his rule and to expand his empire into other lands. Over the next two decades, more and more clans joined his: Tarkuts, Arulats, Manguts, Jalairs, and more. Some people were conquered and others came to him willingly to improve their lives. Temujin always rewarded people who were loyal to him with wealth and power.

Now that he led such a large number of people, Temujin began negotiating alliances with other chieftains. Within a few years, he had united the Mongols, Merkits, Tatars, Naimans, Uighurs, Keraits, and several smaller clans, and they became known collectively as the Mongols. In 1206, these men elected him as the Great Khan, ruler over all the Mongol clans, about 2 million people. He took the name Genghis Khan, the Fierce Ruler.

The Silk Road

In 1207, the Khan began a campaign against the Tanguts of Western Xia, who threatened Mongolia's western border. His first battle against them resulted in a victory, but he still had not captured the nearby city. His army had no way to breach the walls. But he was a clever man and decided to use trickery. He sent a messenger to the Tangut general, saying that he would be willing to leave if he was given a gift of 1000 cats and 10,000 birds. The general was bewildered but happy to end the battle. The animals were rounded up and sent out to the Khan.

Genghis had his men tie small bits of cotton wool and fabric to the tails of all the animals. The fabric was then set on fire and the animals were set free. Terrified, the creatures scattered, running straight for the city and their nests and homes, setting thousands of small fires. The remaining defenders and the civilians in the city rushed to put them all out. The Mongol army stormed in, crushing the last resistance.

City after city fell to the Khan's creative schemes. But he needed to take the capital, Yinchuan, to claim Western Xia for his own. For two months, the Mongol khan tried everything he could think of. Nothing worked. Finally, he tried to use the Yellow River, which ran near the city, to his advantage. His men broke the dykes and tried to flood the city to drive the people out. But the city was built on and surrounded by flatland. Although the water spread out far around, it wasn't deep enough to flood the city. It did, however, wash away the Mongol tents and some horses, forcing the Mongol army to retreat to higher ground.

As Genghis spent weeks considering one plan after another, only to discard them, the flood began to have an unexpected effect. It had ruined the crops around Yinchuan, leaving the people with nothing to eat. With no one to turn to for help, people starving in the city, and the Mongol army camped on their doorstep, the Tanguts surrendered. It had taken almost three years, but Genghis Khan had conquered Western Xia.

His kingdom now straddled the Silk Road, and merchants often stopped to deliver gifts to him. Genghis always made these men welcome. He was anxious to learn as much as he could about the lands outside his own, and he was fascinated by the stories the merchants told. He listened intently when they described China as a place of unimaginable wealth. He often watched the caravans lumbering along the Silk Road, stuffed with silver and gold, luxurious silks and other fabrics, thick furs, and weapons.

He was dismayed by some news, however. The Jin Dynasty, who ruled northern China and had traditionally been the overlords of the Mongol clans, had an army far superior to his own. Genghis tapped his fingers thoughtfully as the traders described giant chariots pulled by teams of horses and weapons that exploded and tore apart anything near them. He knew he would eventually have to face the Jin, and it worried him. Were these merchants exaggerating? He needed to know more!

Military Uses of the Silk Road

Despite their difficulties and dangers, the Silk Road routes were the highways of the east. Military leaders counted on these roads to move troops and supplies quickly. They were the best routes for an attacking army to take, although sometimes a general would move cross-country instead to take an enemy by surprise. Within a country, the Silk Road routes also served military purposes. Chinese warlords often fought one another, sometimes toppling an emperor and setting up a new dynasty. They used the Silk Roads inside China; so did invaders, like Genghis Khan.

He realized then just how important the Silk Road had become to his growing empire. Using the trade routes, his armies could move fast, but, more important, merchants and spies could bring him information about his enemies. He took steps to keep the Silk Road safe, with soldiers patrolling the routes to keep bandits away. Merchants could travel safely, even with precious silks or carved ivory and jade.

After Genghis Khan made the routes safer, patterns of travel changed. Counting on Mongol protection, more travelers made longer trips. They experienced strange weather, ate exotic food, rode beasts they had never seen before, and bought goods made of materials unknown in their homelands. They negotiated their deals by using foreign currency and languages they barely understood. And they continued to stop to pay tribute to the Khan and share their information.

Good roads led to faster travel, meaning traders could move delicate foods much farther than before. Soon, Genghis and his clan were enjoying gifts of grapes, melons, pomegranates, plums, pears, peaches, dates, quinces, and oranges. The fruit was

Genghis Khan used a system of outposts to relay important messages quickly.

Getting the Message Out

The first outpost buildings along the Silk Road were gers. Fresh horses waited for riders at each post to relay messages. The Great Khan's messengers traveled farther and faster than the riders of the famous Pony Express, which carried messages across the American west in 1860, more than 700 years later.

Genghis Khan's successors improved his relay system. Kubilai Khan, emperor of China and grandson of Genghis, worked with the three other Mongol khans to station runners every 5 kilometers (3 miles) all the way from Beijing to Persia—more than 4000 kilometers (2485 miles)! Runners wore bells as a signal so that the next man would be ready and waiting to go. Even in bad weather, important news or messages (about a khan's death, for instance) could travel a distance of 10 days' march in one day and one night. They operated the system around the clock.

cold and fresh, packed in ice taken from the mountain passes. The dark purple, warm orange, and bright red colors of fruit were a wonder to Genghis.

The Khan also spent money to make the routes more easily passable. His armies crossed treacherous mountain passes as readily as they did dangerous deserts, following paths on which pack animals were more common than men. They took laborers on these mountain routes, and under the direction of Chinese engineers, the workers used wedges, hammers, pry bars, and spades to widen the paths. They hewed giant steps into rock faces and hung swaying rope bridges across chasms for caravans to use. They cleared away thick brush and knocked down rocky outcroppings that could give robbers a place to hide.

Now travel was not limited to traders and soldiers. Artists, craftspeople, and others moved from Persia and settled in Mongolia. Tax collectors, census takers, judges, master builders, musicians, scholars, and spies were only some of the folks who might bed down in the same crowded caravanserai.

Genghis Khan reasoned that fast communication was also vital for conquests and for running a government in his large kingdom. He set up a messenger service, called the *yam*, with posts on the east–west routes of the Silk Road. And Genghis learned that, indeed, his merchants were telling the truth about the Jin.

The Empire Expands

When a new emperor was chosen for the Jin Dynasty, he sent a group of ambassadors to Genghis Khan. The Khan granted them an audience, curious about what they might want. An alliance, perhaps?

The men bowed after they were ushered in. "Great Khan, the new Jin emperor has been installed. He demands that you and your people acknowledge him as your overlord. We expect to take with us your tribute to your emperor." A tribute was a huge payment of gold, silver, and other riches. The men stared arrogantly at the Khan, fully expecting him to comply.

Genghis felt a cold wave of rage ripple through him. He stood ramrod straight and pinned the men with his fierce stare. The change in the Khan made the ambassadors take a step back in confusion. The Khan spat at the feet of the men, truly offended by their demand.

"Tell your new emperor that he is a fool!" Genghis sneered as the ambassadors cowered. "His empire is crumbling and his people are starving. He is a puppet emperor!" The new ruler had some 43 million subjects and famine was widespread. "Be grateful that I will let you live to take this message back to him. One day, he will bow to me!" He snapped his fingers and his soldiers hustled the group out of the Great Khan's presence.

Genghis was furious. He paced back and forth in his war room, determined now to take down the Jin. But his army of 75,000 would face more than 2 million Chinese soldiers. He'd need to get into fortified cities. Two huge fortresses would also never fall to a direct attack. The Khan forced himself to overcome his anger. He needed to think clearly so he would not act in haste.

As usual, he went to find Borte and get her advice. He found her out on the grasslands that she loved, near her horses. Mongol women were just as strong riders as the men, and Borte was particularly skilled. As a ruler's wife, she could have let slaves do everything for her, but she enjoyed being independent. He watched for a few moments as she deftly slit animal tendons into long, thin strands. Her nimble fingers quickly rolled and twisted them into long threads.

True Love

Mongol men could have more than one wife, and although Genghis did marry other women later, Borte was always his queen. At any time, he could have installed a new wife as queen, and most rulers did so. But for Genghis, Borte was always his true love. Borte and Temujin had four sons together: Jochi, Chagatai, Ogedei, and Tolui. Their sons and grandsons ruled the empire after the Khan's death.

Later, she would use this thread to sew socks and other pieces of clothing from felt.

He told her about the ambassadors' visit. Borte sighed, knowing her husband would once again be leaving for war. "Temujin," she said, still calling him by the name no one else would dare to use, "you have the advantage of information from the merchants. You know more about the Jin than they do about you. I have heard that several high-ranking Jin members have also defected to us. Seek them out. Offer them protection in return for their secrets."

She smiled at her husband. "Plan for everything that you can think of and allow for what you can't. Use your spies and listen to them carefully."

Genghis gently rubbed Borte's callused hands. "You are right, of course," he said, and he smiled back at her.

After several years of careful planning, Genghis was ready to attack. In 1211, he moved against the Jin Dynasty. He gathered his soldiers in a valley and made sure each had a trio of horses. Despite their small size, Mongolian horses could gallop for 30 kilometers (20 miles) or more without stopping. When one horse tired, the soldier would ride the next one. In this way, the army could move at a top speed without exhausting their mounts. And that would be important, for Genghis planned to push his army 800 kilometers (500 miles) straight across the gravel expanse of the Gobi Desert.

It would be a challenge. In a few places, springs, forests, and steppe lands broke up the plain, but the men would stick to the empty spaces. The enemy would not be watching for them to come from the desert.

The Khan and his army would attack the desert the way they would any enemy: relentlessly and swiftly, but carefully. Once again, Genghis repeated his plans for his generals. "I will lead. Then each of you will follow with a wave of men. We cannot all travel together.

The Gobi Desert

The Gobi Desert covers almost one-third of the southern part of Mongolia. Most of it is a huge plain of gravelly dirt, with some rocky hills and a few oases dotting the landscape. Temperatures in summer can reach 40 degrees Celsius (104 degrees Fahrenheit), and in winter, they drop to a frigid –40 degrees Celsius (–40 degrees Fahrenheit). Less than 100 millimeters (4 inches) of rain fall in a year, and in some parts, rain falls only every two or three years.

One of the few areas with huge sand dunes, some more than 90 meters (295 feet) tall, is the Khongoryn Els, or Singing Sands. Today, it is a popular tourist spot. The "singing" sound is made when massive sheets of loose sand, stirred by the fierce winds, move across more stable sands. It sounds something like the drone of an airplane and can be heard from far away. In spring and fall, winds in the Gobi can reach 140 kilometers (90 miles) per hour, creating a chorus of sand voices.

Another popular tourist spot is Great Gobi National Park, which is larger in area than Switzerland. Many unusual animals live there, including the last remaining wild Bactrian camels (which have two humps), the Gobi bears, or *mazaalai* (which are near extinction and are the only bears that live in a desert), and the Saiga antelope (which has an unusual long and flexible nose that warms the air the animal breathes in the winter and filters out the dust in the summer).

Although this picture illustrates a time after the Great Khan's, it shows how well the Mongols learned to lay siege to walled cities and use catapults.

The Jin were shocked when the Mongols surprised them in the pass: the Mongols had come out of the desert. Surely no army could do that! The suddenness and soundlessness of the attack and the unyielding hail of arrows that rained down caused the Jin to turn and flee. Many at the front trampled their fellow soldiers while trying to escape from the narrow pass. Genghis pushed his troops through them, like a battering ram through a closed door. They took many Chinese soldiers as prisoners, and the Khan had a plan for them. It was the first of Genghis Khan's many small victories over the Jin.

As always, in open spaces and natural surroundings, the Mongols were unstoppable. The Jin retreated to their fortified cities, hoping to wait out the invaders. But the Khan was a man who always worked to overcome his weaknesses, and he had found Chinese engineers among his prisoners. From them, he and his advisers learned about siege warfare. The Mongols built huge triple crossbows that launched 3-meter-long (10-foot-long) arrows that flew as far as 1 kilometer (0.6 miles), shattering walls and ramparts.

Trebuchets, or catapults, were then mounted on wagons. Strong Mongol men quickly hauled on ropes attached to 10-meter (30-foot) levers. Hundreds of boulders, some weighing 2 kilograms (4 pounds) each, were loaded on the other end of the levers to fly up and out. They smashed holes in thick city walls from 200 meters (655 feet) away. The Mongol warriors quickly cut down anyone from neighboring cities bringing wagonloads of food to the besieged city and enjoyed the rations themselves. City after city fell, moving Genghis ever closer to the capital and the emperor. Finally, dispirited and

Written Records

Genghis Khan admired the Chinese bureaucracy so much that he put a Chinese high official, Chu'Tsai, in charge of organizing his Mongol government and records. He needed someone who could create a written set of laws. As nomads, the Mongols had no experience in governing cities and countries. One of Genghis Khan's great strengths was his ability to find the right person for a job and give him the authority and resources to do it well.

As far as we know, Genghis Khan never learned to read or write. Early in his empire building, however, he felt he needed written records. Under his direction, scholars adapted the Turkish alphabet to create—for the first time—a way of writing the Mongolian language. Unfortunately, very little 13th-century Mongolian writing has survived, and much of what we know about the Mongols has come from Chinese records.

The shah knew little about Mongolia and he cared even less. However, rich gifts were always welcome, and more trade meant more taxes for him. He signed the agreement.

Genghis was pleased that everything had gone so smoothly. He may have been an experienced warrior, but he had less experience as a diplomat. He had made alliances only with other nomadic leaders, never a foreign ruler. He assumed his reputation for war must have been known to the shah. Genghis wasted no time in using his new alliance.

The first trade caravan from Mongolia, headed for Samarkand, arrived at the shah's border city of Otrar. The governor was a greedy man. He counted 500 camels in that caravan, all loaded with gold, silver, silk, and fur. Lacking any special instructions from the shah, the governor declared that the people in the caravan party were spies. He had them all executed and kept the cargo.

When the news reached Genghis Khan, he was shocked and saddened to have lost so many people. He believed the shah would honor his agreement and punish his wicked governor. Genghis tried to keep a cool head, and he sent another ambassador to the shah. To make it clear that he wasn't making a threat, the Khan sent only two soldiers with the ambassador. He instructed the ambassador to ask the shah to punish the murderous governor.

When the party returned, the Great Khan flew into a rage. The shah had burned off the hair and beards of the two soldiers. Worse yet, they carried with them the ambassador's severed head.

The Great Khan could feel that old fire burning in him once again. He could not allow such a terrible insult to go unanswered. But, as always, he refused to act in haste. This time, not even Borte could settle him, and he spent three days alone in the mountains, thinking and praying. As he knelt on a summit, the wind tugged

Religion in Mongolia

Genghis Khan respected religions that were different from his own and allowed the conquered peoples of his empire to worship in their own way. Genghis himself remained a Shamanist, worshiping the spirits of all natural things, such as the sun, the moon, the stars, and water. Fire, too, was sacred. Mongol Shamanists believed that Heaven had determined Genghis Khan's future before he was born: he was destined to conquer and to spread a new way of living. His sons were to continue the work of destiny.

at his tunic and made his eyes water. "I did not start this war," he said aloud, "but give me strength to take my vengeance."

Finally, he returned, hardened once again. He sent one last message to the shah: "You have chosen war."

The War Begins

Genghis Khan had learned much from his years of battle. Each time, he remembered what worked and what didn't and fine-tuned his campaign. The Mongols would fight much of this war along the Silk Road routes, out in the open, where they were supreme. But they were ready now for siege warfare too, when the time came.

The shah's army was huge—400,000 men—but they were spread thinly along a very long border. They also still had to worry about revolt among the shah's subjects. But they were confident that they would easily defeat the Mongol army, which was only a quarter the size of theirs.

With all the improvements that the Khan had made to the Silk Road routes, his army easily crossed the Tian Shan Mountains, which had claimed so many lives in the past. When the shah's son, Jalal,

Who Would Lead?

When Genghis decided to move against Khwarezm, some considered it foolish. No nomad leader had ever tried to take over an empire so far away. Khwarezm was at the center of Inner Asia at that time and easily as powerful as the Mongol empire. Fearing that Genghis might be killed, his council asked him about who would succeed him and become the next ruler of the Mongols. Only the Great Council, or Kuraltai, had the power to make the final choice, but they wanted to know who Genghis thought would make the best leader. There was no Mongol tradition favoring the eldest son, and so Genghis nominated his third son, Ogedei.

heard that Mongol warriors had passed the mountains, he went to meet them with 50,000 soldiers.

What he saw when he reached the Mongol army was exactly what Genghis wanted him to see: a force only half as big as his—tired men on tired ponies, battered by the treacherous mountains. Genghis knew the shah's men had never seen Mongols fight, and he had decided to use his favorite trick. When the Mongols saw the advancing army, they turned and rode back the way they had come. It seemed as if they were running away, and the shah's men eagerly galloped after them.

The Mongols, of course, were setting the trap that had succeeded so many times before. As soon as they reached the foothills, they turned and fought with a ferociousness that caught the shah's army off guard. They were unprepared for the Mongols' expertise on horseback and as bowmen. The shah's men were trained with long curved sabers for close-contact hand-to-hand combat with an enemy. They couldn't reach the Mongols, whose arrows flew with deadly accuracy from beyond the reach of a sabre.

Attacking the Mongolian horses wouldn't work either, as most wore their own armor: a large panel on each side stretched from head to tail. The panels were fastened to the saddle, across the neck, and just behind the saddle. Another panel covered the hindquarters, with just a hole for the long tail. A fourth piece acted like a breastplate and was also joined to the side panels. The last piece was an iron plate that protected the animal's forehead.

Many men on both sides died, but at the end of the day the Mongol invaders drew back. The shah thought he had won an easy victory, but it was all part of the Khan's plan. Genghis had ingeniously divided his army into four sections. Each section had a mission to keep part of the shah's army busy.

The second section attacked the city of Otrar, whose governor had seized the Mongol caravan and murdered its people. For five months, the Khan's men laid siege to the city, finally breaching the walls. Soldiers in the city's central fortress kept up the fight for two more months, but eventually Genghis Khan's men captured the governor alive, as ordered. As punishment for the murder and robbery that had sparked this war, the Mongols executed him publicly, pouring molten silver into his eyes and ears until he died.

The third section of the Mongol army had gone south to attack the shah's border and destroy fortifications. The shah sent out his last reserves, keeping only enough men to defend Samarkand, his capital. The Mongol soldiers and their horses were well rested,

When Genghis conquered Bukhara, he insisted that the Kalyan Minaret be kept standing because of its beauty.

from the empty houses. They could not damage the buildings, though, and they must *not* harm the townspeople.

The Khan used plunder to help motivate his troops. He expected a lot from them, but he praised and rewarded those who delivered more than he expected. He punished those who fell short, making sure the punishment fit the crime. One unit commander thought the Khan would ignore his stealing in Bukhara. In the next battle, Genghis demoted him to foot soldier and placed him on the front line, where he was soon killed.

Genghis learned later that the defeated shah had remained on the run, afraid, and sleeping in a different tent every night. Finally, he had reached an island, where he became sick and eventually died. Genghis Khan and his troops then rode south looking for the shah's heir, his son, Jalal, and what was left of the shah's great army. It was autumn. Orchards lined the hilly roads; the heady scents of apples and apricots, almonds, peaches, plums, pomegranates, and melons filled Genghis's nose as he inhaled deeply.

The Khan was conflicted. He usually delegated troops to take control of the lands he passed through, thus safeguarding the rear and securing his men. This time, however, he had no soldiers to spare, but he had to ensure that his enemies did not regroup behind him. Genghis did not like to burn barns and crops, but his own men were his priority. He took a long look over the full orchards and lush fields, and his mouth set in a tight line. On his orders, his soldiers laid waste to the whole region. Everything went up in flames. He knew it was an appalling way to protect his troops, but it was the only one available to him. He could not put his men's lives at risk.

The Mongols caught up with Jalal on the bank of the Indus River in 1221. Jalal fought courageously but in vain. At last he jumped into the river and swam across, still carrying his battle flag. The Khan watched him crawl out on the other side, and he held up his hand. "Let that man go," he ordered. "He is a brave warrior. Let him live."

Along the road back to Samarkand, the country still smelled of burning. The Khan gave water and food to the women, children, and old folk who had remained. They were his people now.

A Reign Ends

Over time, Genghis slowly delegated more authority to his trusted generals and his sons. He spent more time with his beloved Borte. Just as his Mongol armies were poised to strike central Europe in 1227, the Great Khan died. Luckily for Europe, the senior members of the clans had to go home quickly because they were part of the Great Council, the Kuraltai, and would choose the next ruler. The Kuraltai spent almost two years discussing the succession. It was a significant decision: once a Great Khan was chosen, every Mongol was legally obligated to obey him. In 1229, they eventually validated Genghis Khan's choice of Ogedei over his older brother, Chagatai.

The Great Khan had left instructions that his burial place was to be left unmarked. A few trusted, loyal servants took his coffin to central Mongolia, quietly and with little ceremony. Its final resting place was concealed from everyone except the funeral escort. Rather than being buried in a real tomb, Genghis had asked for mausoleums, or white palaces, to be built as shrines to him in places where he had lived at different times. His son Ogedei fulfilled the Khan's request.

Genghis Khan had reunited the Mongol clans into a fighting nation. When he died, he was ruler of the biggest land empire the world has ever known, stretching from Russia in the west to much of China in the east. Genghis had used the Silk Road to achieve military supremacy but while doing

A colorful collection of spices in an Indian market

so, he broke down trade barriers and made the long journeys safer for everyone. He brought new luxury to the previously barren Mongol life, as exotic goods now arrived by the Silk Road: glass from Venice, carved ivory from Africa, mosaics from Constantinople, fresh fruits, spices, and perfumes from India. In the time of the Great Khan and Mongol Empire, the Silk Road flourished.

Looking for Genghis Khan's Grave

Even today, nobody knows exactly where the bones of Genghis Khan lie. Before 2000, archeologists had not done much work in Mongolia, but in 2001 a Japanese and Mongolian team unearthed the ruins of a mausoleum. After finding marks of fire and bones of horses, the team felt that it was the mausoleum of Genghis Khan. A memorial service described in Chinese historical records includes mention of fire and horses being buried there.

They also found earrings, brooches, and incense burners with a dragon design, which was the symbol of an emperor. The incense burners match a description in a 14th-century Persian book of history, which says that incense was always kept burning in the Khan's crypt.

If this was the Khan's tomb, then, according to one legend, his grave lies within a 12-kilometer (7-mile) radius of this site. Another legend says that the ancient Mongols diverted a river over the Great Khan's grave so that it will never be found.

"There had to have been a great deal of interaction between east and west at the time, in terms of culture and the exchange of goods," Shinpei Kato, the leader of the Japanese archeologists, told reporters in October 2004. "If we find what items were buried with [Genghis Khan], we could write a new page for world history."

The Description of the World

Marco Polo, a merchant, later wrote a book about his travels, many of which took him along the Silk Road. Marco's book has several titles: *The Description of the World, The Travels of Marco Polo the Venetian,* and *Il Milione.* Whatever title it has, Marco's book is one of the most important ever written. It made Europeans see that a wide world lay beyond their borders.

Marco's book is not a diary that records each day's travel and his personal experiences. Instead, it describes the trading practices of each region he visited. For Marco, trade on the Silk Road was more important than his own story or the people he met.

Marco stared at the dying man and rubbed his trembling hands on his tunic. He had longed to go on this adventure with his father and uncle, to go to China, but he hadn't thought about the dangers. Was he ready to face them?

The Early Years

Marco Polo was born around 1254 in Venice, which is in Europe, at the northern end of the Adriatic Sea. Marco's father, Nicolo, and his Uncle Maffeo were noblemen and wealthy merchants. They spent long stretches of time away from home buying and selling goods. The Polos traded mostly precious gems and jewelry.

Marco's world changed forever when his beloved mother died. As the boy cried for her, he wondered what would happen to him. His father had left on a trip a long time ago, and Marco barely remembered him. He didn't know whether his father was still alive or would ever come back for him. Now he had lost his mother too. Where would he live? Who would look after him?

Who Was Marco Polo?

Because Marco Polo wrote about his travels and not about his own life, we don't know much about him when he was young. We don't know the exact year he was born or his mother's name. We do know that she died during the years that Marco's father was away in China. Marco wasn't well known during his lifetime, and scholars did not take his book seriously, no matter how popular it became. Other people didn't write much about Marco either. In the 16th century, a man named Giovanni Battista Ramusio finally did write about Marco. He tried to find out as much as he could about Marco's life. Much of what we know about the traveler comes from Ramusio. He also published part of Marco's book, along with travel stories from other explorers.

His Uncle Marco, after whom he was named, came to see him. "Marco," his uncle said kindly, "I know you are sad. Naturally, you miss your parents."

Marco kept his gaze on the floor and squeezed his eyes shut tightly to stop the tears. He had promised himself he would be brave if his uncle was going to send him away to live with strangers.

Uncle Marco reached out, tucked his hand under the young boy's chin, and turned his face up. "Would you like to come and live with us?" he asked.

Marco nodded fast, but he didn't trust himself to speak. He was so relieved. Uncle Marco had been like a father while his own was away, and the boy loved him and his family.

"It will mean coming into the family business," Uncle Marco explained. "You will need to learn about trading. I will put you to work right away."

Marco just kept nodding. He would be glad to be a merchant. Being merchants had made the whole Polo family rich. They also helped run the city government.

Marco moved to his uncle's house. Marco's young cousin and his new wife moved into Marco's old house. Over the next few years, Marco learned Latin and some Greek from his uncle, his cousins, and his tutors. He learned French and Italian words that would help in the trading business. He also learned about money and measurements in Venice and other countries. His family was Roman Catholic, and he was taught about religion by their priest.

Marco enjoyed learning while he worked. His uncle had a stall near the busy seaport in Venice. Every day, the stall was filled with people: sailors, traders from other countries, and people who lived in Venice. The traders would bargain with Marco's uncle, wanting him to buy their scented spices from India, rich fabrics from China, and skillfully carved ivory from Africa.

Sailors came to buy salt, wood, and wheat. Sometimes they would buy the delicate colored glass that Venice was famous for, to take back to their homelands. Marco loved to perch on a high stool while his uncle did business. Marco's job was to write down in a book each sale and purchase his uncle made. Marco would scratch away with a quill pen, carefully making the entries and writing receipts. At the end of each day, he would proudly show his uncle his neat printing and long columns of black numbers.

Wielding Weapons

Even though he was still a boy, Marco would have learned to use weapons. All Venetian men and boys were expected to help defend their city. They learned how to shoot crossbows from masters. They had to practice shooting at targets. The men and boys trained in groups of 12. Three times a year, they competed for prizes. Marco likely also learned to fight with a sword.

City of Canals

Venice is built on more than 100 small islands that are in a big lagoon, which is like a saltwater lake. The city is surrounded by canals and has about 400 bridges. In the oldest parts of the city, the canals are the roads—no cars are allowed and people do a lot of walking on the paved sidewalks. Many of the canals in Venice are natural ones. Some were dug later to make it easier to get around. In Marco's time, people used gondolas, a type of boat, as transportation. Today, gondolas are still used by tourists, but most Venetians use motorized boats, water buses, or water taxis.

To build on the marshy islands, millions of wooden posts, called piles, were used to support the foundations of buildings. These piles were hammered through the soft sand and mud into the hard bedrock at the bottom of the lagoon. Amazingly, the piles remain preserved to this day. They never rot because oxygen can't reach them underwater, and, over the centuries, minerals in the water have helped to make the piles as hard as stone.

"Bravo, Marco, very good," Uncle Marco would say as he patted his nephew on the back. "You always do such a fine job." Sometimes his uncle would reward him with an extra coin or two. Sometimes it was a silver grosso. If he had done very well, it might even be a gold ducat!

Venice, where Marco lived, was a city of canals, built on marshy islands. Venice and its rival, Genoa, were the two great European centers of trade with the Middle East. From the eastern shore of the Mediterranean Sea, they shipped goods by water or by land on the Silk Road.

Whenever he had free time, Marco went to the harbor to see the ships arriving from all over Europe and lands to the east. He would try to talk to the sailors and merchants in their own languages and learn more from them. They spoke many different languages. They were happy to teach words to Marco, if he helped with the unloading.

The Silk Road and the Merchant

As the boy lifted boxes and stacked crates, the men shared stories about where they had been and the amazing things they had seen. Marco was fascinated. He dreamed of heading out on an Eastern trading mission as soon as he was old enough.

By now Marco was 13 years old. His father and his Uncle Maffeo had left on a trading mission seven years earlier, and the Polo family was sure they must be dead. No one had heard from them since they left. And yet Marco found himself looking for his family on each ship that came into the harbor. Wouldn't it be wonderful if they did return? What thrilling stories of their travels they would tell.

A Father's Journey

In fact, although they had no way to get a message home to their family, Marco's father, Nicolo, and his Uncle Maffeo were very much alive. They had spent some time in Constantinople (which is now Istanbul, in Turkey). When they traded the things they had brought from Venice, people paid for them with jewels. The men went through Crimea and continued to a Mongol city on the Volga River. The ruler there had never seen such wonderful jewels! Traders from Turkey didn't often go that far east. He traded everything the Polos had for things that were worth much, much more.

The Merchants of Venice

Many merchants like Marco's father and Uncle Maffeo traveled and did business for themselves. Traders from Venice had to start out by sea, but they often continued by land to Egypt and east on the Silk Road. Merchants often had to be away from their homes for years at a time. The merchants of Venice were very well known around the world. In the late 16th century, William Shakespeare wrote a play called *The Merchant of Venice.*

The Polos were happy with their trade mission and wanted to go back home to Venice. They could sell the Mongol goods for lots of money there. But war had broken out and it wasn't safe to go back the way they had come. The brothers joined a caravan traveling farther east, hoping to reach the ocean and sail back to Venice.

In Bukhara (north of Afghanistan), the Polos met some men at a caravanserai. These men were messengers, headed for China. The Polos were excited—on the Silk Road, they had met many interesting people, but never anyone going to China. Some people in Europe at that time thought the world was flat and China was at its very edge. Hardly anyone from Europe had been there. The Polos had so many questions for the men that the messengers invited them to come to the court of the great Kubilai Khan, emperor of China.

The Polos' journey to China took them along the Silk Road through Samarkand and Kashgar. They finally arrived at Kubilai's court in Sheng-du in 1266. Kubilai Khan was very curious about Venice and Europe. He spent a lot of time talking with the Polos. He got the idea that the pope, who is the head of the Roman Catholic Church, was the most powerful ruler in Europe, even more powerful than the kings. Kubilai wanted to develop an alliance with him. The Great Khan was a Buddhist, but his mother had been a Christian

These ancient temples and graves in Samarkand were built starting in the 11th century, though little remains from that time. Most date from between the 13th and 15th centuries.

and he was interested in that religion. The emperor gave Marco's father and uncle letters to take to the pope.

The emperor also gave the Polos several oblong golden tablets. These heavy plaques would help keep the traders safe in China and the entire Mongol Empire. In return, the Polos were to bring back 100 Christian priests to teach the Chinese people about Christianity, and some holy oil from Jerusalem. The oil was from a special church and was said to have magical powers. Kubilai wanted to use it against his enemies.

With the emperor's tablets to smooth the way, the Polos traveled in luxury through Asia, and then took a ship to Venice. Marco's father was looking forward to seeing his son and wife again at last. It was a terrible shock when he went to his house only to find other family members living there. They sent Nicolo straight to Uncle Marco's. Nicolo was crushed to learn about his wife's death but elated to meet his son there.

Soon, Marco was spending every evening listening to the stories Nicolo and Maffeo told of China and the Great Khan's kingdom. Marco shared his own stories too. Nicolo was so impressed by his son and everything the boy had learned that he invited him to join the family's next mission to China.

The Golden Tablets

Kubilai Khan's golden tablets were called *paizas* or *paidzse* in Venice. The word was based on the Chinese word *p'ai-tzu*, meaning "tablets of authority." The heavy tablets were 30 centimeters (12 inches) long and 9 centimeters (4 inches) wide and were engraved with the royal symbol. Some tablets were shaped like tigers or falcons at the top, while others were plain rectangles. Travelers who carried the tablets were under the Great Khan's protection. The tablets gave permission to officials throughout his empire to provide any boats, horses, lodging, food, and guides the travelers asked for.

The Great Khan

Kubilai Khan was one of Genghis Khan's grandsons. In 1260, he became the Great Khan of all the Mongols, as Genghis had been. In 1271, he created the Yuan Dynasty, which ruled Mongolia and part of China. By 1279, he had driven the Song Dynasty from the rest of China and become the emperor of all of China. Kubilai liked Chinese culture. He wore Chinese clothes and ate Chinese food (although he never learned the language). He tried to do all the things a Chinese emperor would do. But like Mongol rulers, Kubilai kept himself in good shape. His grandfather had warned him that a life built on pleasure had made Chinese rulers soft and easy to conquer.

Kubilai did many good things for China, such as creating jobs, fixing buildings, making highways, and rebuilding the Grand Canal. He supported Chinese artists. He believed people should be free to follow any religion they chose.

Kubilai had four wives, but Empress Chabi was his favorite. She was an ardent Buddhist, and she encouraged Kubilai to adopt her beliefs and make Buddhism the most important religion in his empire. The Chinese people liked her. She helped Kubilai and the former Chinese royal family to make agreements. Without her, they would have tried to overthrow the Khan, or the Khan would have destroyed them. Chabi helped to arrange marriages to build trust.

When Chabi died, Kubilai lost his main link with his Chinese subjects. Chabi's son, and Kubilai's chosen heir, died shortly after his mother. Kubilai never really got over their deaths, and his strong grip on the country and on his health slowly slipped away. He died in 1294.

time teaching Marco to speak one more language: Persian. In many Asian lands, Persian was spoken in the markets.

They knew Kubilai Khan would be wondering whether they had failed. The Polos had to go back now if they wanted to set up a trade route with China. Doing so would make them even richer! With great excitement, they planned their return. They spent weeks gathering supplies, including foods like cheese and salted meats (which would not rot); items they could sell, like jewels, beautiful Venetian glass, wood, wine, and woolen cloth; gold ducats and silver grossos to spend; clothing; gifts for the Khan; and even horses.

Finally, in the spring of 1271, Nicolo, Maffeo, and Marco loaded everything onto a big ship and set off. They went first to Jerusalem for the special oil. As they were getting ready to leave again, they heard in the markets that the cardinals had chosen a new pope. The three Venetians turned back to deliver the Khan's letters and ask for the 100 priests. Marco was frustrated by the delay, but he tried to keep his grumbling quiet.

The best the new pope could do was to send two friars. A friar is like a priest, but he serves a community rather than staying in a church. The pope wrote a reply to Kubilai Khan, telling him that the friars could train the Khan's men to become priests. He also sent some special gifts, like crystal vases and goblets. The Polos and the friars set sail again in November on the Mediterranean Sea, planning to land in Armenia.

Armenia was the best place to start their journey by land. Set right by the port was the city of Ayas's busy market, and merchants from Venice, Genoa, and Pisa made frequent trips there. Goods from all over the Middle East were brought to Ayas. Everyone going on a trading journey inland started there. But when the Polos' ship reached the Armenian port, they and the friars found the city in an uproar. As quickly as they could, they bundled up their goods and food and loaded their packhorses.

The Journey

Beijing, China's capital, is almost 8900 kilometers (5530 miles) from Venice. The Polos had a very long way to go. After leaving Jerusalem, they sailed to Armenia. Leaving there, they went to Hormuz on the Persian Gulf, doubled back to Kerman, and then headed north to Afghanistan. From there, they traveled through a desert to the city of Cobinan and then on to Persia. Their route took them east to Balkh and through the Hindu Kush and Pamir mountains to Kashgar. Their next stop was Khotan, before they crossed the Gobi Desert. Finally, they reached northern China.

Construction of the Lugou Bridge was completed in 1192 and it was reconstructed in 1698. Highly praised by Marco Polo during his visit to China, it is sometimes called the Marco Polo bridge.

"Everything is ready." Nicolo said at last, to Marco's relief. "Now, let's be on our way." Nicolo took a last look around the pier to make sure they had not missed any of their gear. The packhorses were heavily burdened, but Nicolo was sure they could carry everything.

They saddled their riding horses, then mounted and rode swiftly away from the city, headed toward Hormuz. Nicolo kept Marco close by his side. The two friars, however, had had enough. Too much in this journey had been strange to them. They longed for the kind of life they knew, for familiar foods and clothes, and above all for people more like themselves. When the party met a group of monks headed for Jerusalem, the friars decided to join them and leave the Polos.

The Polos looked at one another and took stock. Marco could see the worry etched on the older men's faces, and he fiddled with the edge of his tunic. They had no religious men to present to Kubilai Khan. Would the holy oil, letters, and presents from the pope be enough? Would the Great Khan welcome them back at court? Would he banish them from China—or worse? Nicolo closed his eyes and clenched his teeth. For the first time, he wondered whether he had made the right choice in bringing his only son on such a dangerous journey.

Heading South

"We need to push on," Maffeo said, pulling thoughtfully on his long beard. "We need to open that route to China, and all the lands the Silk Road passes through, if we are to trade with the Far East. There is a lot of money to be made, and we need the Khan on our side. Not facing him at all would close those doors for good, brother."

Nicolo looked at Marco for a moment and nodded. They would go on. Marco let out the breath he hadn't even realized he was holding. He would have done just about anything not to have to go home.

Making Money

In Marco's time, most merchants would travel to another city and sell their goods there. Another merchant would take those goods to another town and sell them for a little more money than he had paid for them. Another merchant would do the same. By the time the goods had gone all the way to China, they were very expensive. If the Polos could sell their Venetian goods in China, they could charge high prices and keep all the profit. They would do the same thing on the way back. They could bring soft silks from China; diamonds, rubies, and pearls from other countries; spices from Indonesia; and carpets from Turkey. If they could get them all safely home, they could sell them and be very rich!

The Polos joined other merchants headed southeast toward Hormuz on the Persian Gulf. Along the way, the large party stopped at many trading centers and markets. They did a lot of business in the crowded bazaars and spent the nights in comfort at local caravanserais. At night, after a good meal, they settled themselves around the fire and the older Polos traded information with other travelers.

While they were busy, Marco wrote in the journals he was keeping. He noted the goods available and needed in each region, and which markets were best for each item. He also wrote about any dangers and the best places to get supplies, including water. Sitting with his family, he would take a deep lungful of air, trying to memorize the smells and sights of each place. Sometimes he wrote late into night, after the others had gone to bed and the fire had dwindled to embers.

When they stopped in Kerman, on the Persian border, the Polos stocked up on riding gear and weapons: saddles, bridles, spurs, swords, bows, and quivers were for sale. People in Kerman also bred falcons to hunt with. No matter how swift the prey, the fierce-looking birds always caught it. The Polos feasted on the unlucky pheasants and partridges, happily licking the grease from their fingers.

dates, pomegranates, and quinces spread out for kilometers. All the towns along this part of the Silk Road were surrounded by thick, high mud walls for defense against raiders. The land was crisscrossed by streams, and parrots and other bright-colored birds shone against the date palms, their cries piercing the quiet.

Finally the travelers reached the ocean shore. Hormuz was on a nearby island. Although all its water had to be brought over from the mainland, Hormuz had become a great city in which traders from India sold their amazing wares: spices and drugs, precious stones, pearls, gold cloth, and elephants' ivory tusks. Marco gladly went to work buying and selling in the market, watched closely by Nicolo and Maffeo. The men were proud of Marco's abilities and how quickly he learned the trading language in measures in each region. Marco was quite excited to be getting rich as they traveled.

Battling Deserts

The Polos were planning to sail from Hormuz to India. They went down to the waterfront to find a ship to rent. When they arrived at the port, the ships they saw didn't look like any they were used to. Marco touched the hull of one and was surprised at how hard the wood was. It was so hard, in fact, that nails couldn't be hammered into it. Instead, Marco saw wooden dowels holding all the planks together. He looked closer and saw fibers twining in and out.

"Father, Uncle, surely these ships could not weather a storm," Marco said with a frown. "They would just come apart!" He shook his head and pointed to the ropes tying the ships to the pier. "The boats don't even have iron anchors."

"True, but we've traveled on similar boats before,"

Maffeo replied, running his hand along the rough hull of one ship. "What other option do we have?"

"When we traveled before," Nicolo reminded his brother, "we did not have Marco with us. I am not certain I want to trust my son's life to these vessels." He thought for a few moments and sighed. "The only choice is to go back to Kerman and head northwest from there. There is a route, but it will lead us through deserts." He smiled at his son. "Better to chance a fiery desert than a watery grave."

Marco felt a little knot in his stomach. Burning in the desert or drowning? He hadn't imagined his trip would be filled with choices like these. "The sands it is," he said, swallowing his fear.

They set out and soon encountered a huge desert, the first on their journey. They hired guides to see them through, stocked up on water, and exchanged their horses for camels. During the day, Marco's head swam as the heat shimmered in waves off the endless dunes. At night, he shivered in his bedroll as the sweat of the day dried in the cool night air. Riding in the stiff wooden seat on the camel made his back ache and his thighs sore.

For the first few days, they found very little water, so they drank sparingly. When they finally saw a pond in the distance, the Polos ran toward it.

"Stop!" yelled one of their guides. "Do not drink that water. One sip of it will rot your gut." He shook his head hard. "We will *not* carry three sick men through the desert."

Marco quickly withdrew his hand from the pond. They weren't able to stop the camels, though. They drank their fill of the thick green water. Soon, each animal had diarrhea. The rest of the trip was a smelly one. Every man kept a good distance from the others' animals as they rode.

On the fourth day, the travelers came to a freshwater river. Men and beasts gratefully drank and bathed in its streams, letting it wash

Oxygen at High Altitudes

The higher the altitude, the less oxygen the air has. We call that air *thin*. Near the peak of the Pamir Mountains, at a very high altitude, the air was very thin. Burning is called a *combustion process*, which is a chemical reaction. A combustion process needs oxygen. In turn, it releases heat and light in the form of flames. The more oxygen a fire has, the hotter it gets. At high altitudes, with less oxygen available, the flames don't get as big or as hot as they normally would. Even water boils at a lower temperature, so all food takes a long time to cook.

The party finally descended to the city of Kashgar. Even the weak sun felt warm after the bitter cold of the mountains. The yaks happily shook the snow and ice from their long hair. Marco turned his face up and closed his eyes as he rode. He could smell spring in the air.

The north and south Silk Road routes met in Kashgar. The city was sandwiched between the cold Pamir Mountains and the hot Taklamakan Desert. Whether crawling out from the desert or thawing out after crossing the mountains, travelers could find in Kashgar whatever they needed for the rest of their journey.

People of every description crammed themselves into Kashgar's lively bazaar, and Marco was there with them. Local merchants competed with traders from India, China, Persia, and other far-flung countries to shout the loudest and make the best deals. They haggled over livestock, beautiful fabrics and rich furs, lumps of jade, woven rugs, and daggers and knives encrusted with jewels. Marco eagerly made deals while munching on the sweet and fragrant local melons. He sold the mirrors from Cobinan and bought nutmeg, pepper, and cinnamon from India and the Spice Islands. He felt a little thrill each time he made a good trade.

Animals Were Important

Most people used camels and horses on the Silk Road, but yaks, oxen, donkeys, and mules also carried people and pulled carts. Sometimes, a few elephants lumbered along, carrying giant loads. What animals were used depended on what part of the Silk Road the traveler was on. In the northern steppes, heavy four-wheeled wagons were drawn by horses or oxen. Throughout northern China, travelers used a horse and light cart. Sure-footed, long-haired yaks were the animals best suited to cold mountain heights.

When the roads were lost to the desert sands, camels were the first choice. Each one can carry about 225 kilograms (500 pounds) of supplies. Camels can go two weeks without water. Their wide feet help keep them from sinking into the sand. During sandstorms, camels can close their nostrils, and their long eyelashes help keep sand out of their eyes. In a caravan, 50 or more camels were often connected by a rope, with the head of one camel tied to the tail of the one ahead of it.

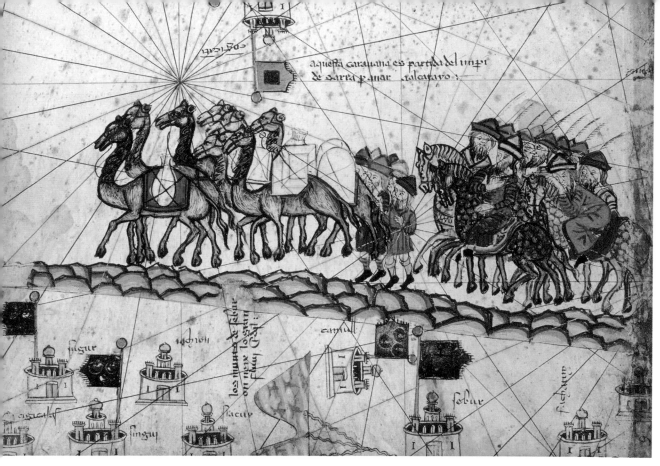

Marco's book became very important to mapmakers. This image from a 14th-century map shows the Polos traveling in their desert caravan.

"Father!" he yelled. "Maffeo! I can't see you. Help me!" Now he could hear music, a gentle tinkling sound. "Father!" His voice rose almost to a screech as he began to panic.

The tinkling grew louder. He turned and a bright light flared in his eyes, blinding him. "Marco." Now he was sure he heard his own name. He was too afraid to move. "Marco!" A hand suddenly touched his shoulder. He let out a strangled scream.

"Marco, it's me, your father!" The hand held him tightly. "It's me! It's okay. Where is your torch? Your camel must have wandered a bit. And you've forgotten to put the bells around his neck. We need those to find each other when this happens. Come now. Let me lead your camel back."

Marco was gripping the reins so tightly that his knuckles were white. He didn't trust himself to speak. The tinkling—of course, that was the bells the camels wore. What had he been thinking? Demons indeed. He shook his head and took in a ragged breath. He felt a little silly now. Nicolo never said a word about how scared Marco had been.

As the days and nights wore on, Marco grew tired of the desert diet of salted meat, hard bread, and cheese, with only water to drink. He was cold at night, but the chilly air felt good after the heat of the day. Moving ahead kept him warm. Marco now always made sure his camel wore its bells and his torch was burning brightly. The guides showed him how the stars that pricked the black sky actually made a map. They used the stars to find their way through the endless wasteland.

It did take them a month to cross almost 1000 kilometers (620 miles) of desert and reach northern China. As they left the sands, they saw a huge group of people coming toward them.

"Marco, come over beside me," Nicolo said. He motioned Maffeo to his other side. The camels spat and grunted while they waited. "Is it bandits? Can you see?" Nicolo asked.

Each man shaded his eyes with his hand, straining to see who was on the road ahead. Dust clouds swirled, hiding the newcomers' faces. Their desert guides, having already been paid, seemed to quietly melt away, leaving the Polos alone to face the crowd.

The Polos moved off the road, staying together in a tight knot. With their loaded camels, they couldn't run and hide. They would have to face whatever this was. As the group came closer, they could see men dressed in silk of every color: orange, red, black, yellow— every man wearing silk! The Polos exchanged stunned glances. Silk was very expensive in Venice.

Slowly banners came into view, as did the small muscular horses the men rode. The men's sun-browned faces creased into smiles as they saw the Polos. Their dark almond-shaped eyes were bright and friendly.

"Kubla Khan"

In 1797, a man named Samuel Coleridge wrote a poem, called "Kubla Khan." It was published in 1816 and became quite famous. Here are opening lines:

In Xanadu did Kubla Khan
A stately pleasure-dome decree:
Where Alph, the sacred river, ran
Through caverns measureless to man
Down to a sunless sea.

It is a long poem, but Coleridge never actually finished it. While he was writing, someone came knocking on his door. When Coleridge sat down to write again later, he couldn't remember what he wanted to write.

Coleridge took a drug called opium, which was legal in his time and is illegal now. The drug sometimes gave him vivid dreams or hallucinations. He had taken some opium and had a daydream while reading Marco Polo's book and the description of the Khan's summer palace. The summer palace at Sheng-du was the Xanadu of Samuel Taylor Coleridge's poem.

Serving the Khan

The Khan studied the men for a few moments. "Rise," he said. He was silent as he looked into the faces of the men before him. Marco shifted his weight from one foot to the other. Suddenly, Kubilai smiled. "I bid you welcome! I was no longer sure that you would return at all. I will accept your presents and letters most gratefully."

The Polos all let out their breath in a rush.

"I am disappointed that the religious men did not accompany you." He pursed his lips thoughtfully. "But I understand how it is when rulers change. You have done your best to fulfill the mission I set for you. Truly, you are loyal men."

He snapped his fingers and several servants appeared from all directions. "Prepare a feast to welcome these men back to China." He waved his hands, sending the servants scurrying to create a lavish meal. "You will all, of course, stay here in the palace with me. I want to hear about your travels and what you have seen."

During the banquet and the days that followed, Marco studied Kubilai whenever he could. Kubilai was twice Marco's age. He was about average height and had pale skin and shining black eyes. To Marco, the Khan seemed to be the perfect ruler: smart, open-minded, tough, decisive, and just.

Kubilai and Marco liked each other right away, and the Polos made their home at Kubilai's wonderful court. The Khan was happy to have the Polos stay with him. Soon, he was confiding in Marco.

"I don't have many people I really trust here at court," he explained while the two sipped tea one afternoon. "I am always certain my Chinese subjects must be plotting to take their country back from me. After all" he smiled at Marco and his black eyes twinkled— "that's what I would do. I keep a Mongol spy network that tells me everything important that happens in my kingdom."

So that's how he knew when we were arriving! Marco thought to himself. He was disappointed to learn that his new friend didn't have special powers.

The Khan let Nicolo and Maffeo travel in his kingdom and do their own trading. Sometimes they were gone for months. Marco spent most of his time with the Khan. Because he was smart and could speak several languages, Marco became a favorite of the emperor's and was given good jobs. At different times, the Khan asked him to work as a tax collector, a census taker, and a supervisor. Sometimes Marco even spied for him.

Marco's jobs for the Khan let him travel all over the Silk Road to remote places in China, to northern Burma, and even to India. The emperor liked to hear interesting details about the places and people Marco saw. He gave his reports to Kubilai in person, not on paper, and he always came back with exciting stories. He loved to entertain the Khan while informing him, too.

Sometimes, though, his job was dangerous. When he was in Tibet, Marco saw some city ruins and wanted to see them up close. He left his escort, who told him the ruins were haunted, and went alone.

Night was just beginning to fall. Marco tried to walk as softly as he could. He couldn't hear another living soul and even his breathing seemed loud here. The silence was eerie, but Marco thought the ruined city had a strange beauty. He closed his eyes and stood still in silence, just inside the walls of what had likely once been someone's home.

He began to have the feeling that he wasn't alone. His eyes flew open, but he stayed still. He couldn't see well in the dim light, and he hadn't brought a torch. It was time to go home. He stepped outside the walls just in time to see a massive tiger silently prowling the streets ahead of him. The animal held its huge head high, as if smelling something in the air. Marco prayed it wasn't him!

Marco figured the big cat weighed almost 200 kilograms (440 pounds). As it walked, the fading light dappled its body. With its dark stripes over orange fur, it almost seemed to disappear some-times. As quietly as he could, Marco quickly went the opposite way from the fierce hunter. This would make a great story for the Khan.

Another time, his group passed close to a swampy lake in southeast Asia. As they stopped to let the horses drink, what looked like a log on the edge of the bank opened its eyes. Marco leapt back and almost tripped. The log was really a horrible, scaly snake—but this snake had four squat legs with three claws on each foot. Marco hid

Crocodiles

What Marco saw was a crocodile. Crocodiles are reptiles that live in warm climates in Africa, Asia, Australia, and parts of the Americas. The species is believed to be 200 million years old—that means they were here before the dinosaurs.

Crocodiles come in many sizes, from just 1 meter (3 feet) to almost 5 meters (16 feet) long. The *Guinness Book of World Records* lists the largest living crocodile, which lives in India in a wildlife sanctuary, as 7 meters (23 feet) long! Crocodiles can weigh more than 1200 kilograms (2646 pounds). The oldest crocodile in the world is likely Mr. Freshy, who lives at the Australia Zoo and is more than 130 years old.

After crocodiles lay their eggs, the temperature the eggs are kept at determines whether male or female babies hatch. Males are born when eggs are around 31.5 degrees Celsius (88.7 degrees Fahrenheit), and females develop at lower and higher temperatures.

behind his horse as the thing opened its massive jaws with a hiss. Peeking around his horse's neck, Marco saw the rows of razor-sharp teeth. Surely this thing could swallow a man whole! Quick as a flash, the beast turned and slipped into the water with barely a ripple. Marco was surprised that something so large—the animal was 10 paces long—could move so fast. His escort told him stories of the ferocious monsters eating lion cubs that ventured too close to their watery homes.

In the 17 years that Marco served the Khan, the thing that fascinated him the most about China was paper money. The first time someone tried to pay him with paper money, Marco thought it was a joke. The Venetians had never seen paper used as money, but everyone in Kubilai's empire used it. The merchants were astonished.

The Silk Road and the Merchant •

143

Paper Money

Although this banknote is from the Ming Dynasty, it is very similar to the ones that thrilled Marco.

Paper money had been used in China for 1000 years before the Polos arrived. Chinese paper was made from fibers in the bark of mulberry trees—the same trees whose leaves fed silkworms.

In Venice and most of Europe in Marco's time, people didn't have paper. They used materials called parchment and vellum. Parchment was made from dried sheepskin and goatskin and was expensive. Vellum was made from calfskin, kidskin, or lambskin and was even more expensive than parchment. Money was never printed on these. Parchment and vellum were used just for writing. Both were much harder to make than Chinese paper.

They began to use paper money, and Marco liked it better. It was much lighter and easier to carry and hide than gold or gems.

Marco made a lot of money working for the Khan, and Nicolo and Maffeo were rich from all the trading they had done. Other people at court became jealous of the Polos as the years passed. By now, Kubilai was almost 80 years old and his health wasn't good. He had already lived much longer than most people did in Marco's time.

The Polos got together to talk one afternoon. They sat in Marco's beautiful apartment in the palace, sipping hot tea from delicate porcelain cups. A warm fire roared and thick Turkish rugs on the marble floor kept their feet warm. "Many here at court would like to see us gone," Nicolo pointed out.

"True," Maffeo nodded. "And if the emperor dies, we may be imprisoned or even killed. No one will protect us."

The three men decided that it was time for them to go home. But they would need the Khan's permission.

Trying to Leave

Over the next three years, the Polos asked several times for permission to leave China. Instead, the emperor gave them more gold, better trade routes, and even land. He was desperate to keep his friends. Marco did his best to explain why they felt they had to leave, but the Khan waved him away. He seemed hurt that the Polos wanted to go. The Polos could not try to sneak out of China. The Mongol's spies would report them.

Marco had now spent almost half his life in China. He might have lived out his years there, except that Queen Bolgana, the Mongol wife of Arghun, Khan of Persia, died in 1287. Her dying wish had been that Arghun would marry another Mongol lady, so Arghun sent three messengers to Kubilai to ask for a bride. Seventeen-year-old Princess Kokachin was chosen.

But getting her to Persia would be difficult. Genghis Khan's grandsons had begun fighting again, so the land routes of the Silk Road were no longer safe. The princess would have to travel by sea.

The Polos saw their chance. Marco had just returned from a trip to India and he knew the route the ships would have to take. He would be a perfect guide for the princess. He went to find the Khan and talk to him.

He found Kubilai in his large throne room with three Persian men. "Great Khan, grant me an audience, please." Marco bowed

The Silk Road by Sea

The Silk Road now included sea routes, which started in China. One branch went across the South China Sea, through the Malacca Straits to India, Arabia, and Persia, and then on to the Persian Gulf and the Red Sea. The other branch led down the East African coast to Tanzania. The Polos' route took them along the coast of Vietnam, around the Malaysian Peninsula, and into the islands of Indonesia.

ship's rail, a feeling of satisfaction filled him. He was going home as a wealthy and well-traveled man.

The Polos' group arrived in Sumatra in April, but the approaching monsoon season kept them from trying to cross the Bay of Bengal. The ships stayed in port for five months. Although Marco had seen many wondrous things in China, in Sumatra he saw many more. When someone gave him one of the large fiber-covered brown nuts that grew on trees, he was astonished at its hardness. The nut had to be smashed open with a hammer. When it was, Marco was told he could drink the sweet milky water that came out. It was wonderful! He also found the white flesh inside surprisingly good, although it was a little tough to chew. He had never seen a food like that before. He learned later that it was called a coconut.

On one trip inland, Marco was sure he saw a unicorn. The animal was grayish-white. Marco could see one long horn coming up from the top of its snout. Later he learned it had a second, shorter horn hidden behind the longer one. It was certainly not a unicorn. This beast had a tough hide, and it didn't have hooves or the beauty of a horse. It lumbered through the grasses on stumpy legs, hairless except for a little bristly tail. It was a white rhinoceros, the world's second-largest land animal alive today, after elephants.

After the monsoon season passed, the group set sail for India. By the time they reached that country's west coast, the 1293 monsoon season had hit. They had to stay ashore again. In India, Marco would go on a boat to watch brave men called pearl divers do their job. Merchants hired the men to dive deep into the ocean and collect pearls. Marco marveled at how long these men could hold their breath. They often dove more than 30 meters (100 feet) into the dark waters. Dives that deep are dangerous, and Marco saw some men drown. Some were also injured or killed by sharks and other creatures. Marco then understood why pearls were so rare and worth so much money.

The group finally boarded their ships, reaching the Persian Gulf and the port of Hormuz that winter. Two of the Persian men had died during the journey. The three Polos and the one surviving Persian took the princess and her attendants by land to North Persia. When they arrived, Arghun's son, Prince Ghazan, told them that King Arghun had died. The young Mongol princess married Prince Ghazan instead. More bad news followed when a messenger brought word to the prince that Kubilai Khan had also died.

Nine months later, the Polos started the final leg of their journey by land. Without their letters and golden tablets from Kubilai Khan, they might not have made it home. Bandits were everywhere. But the Khan's protection outlived him. The Polos often had an escort of 200 or more mounted troops as they traveled through Persia and Armenia to Trebizond on the Black Sea.

The huge Venetian warship that Marco commanded had 120 oars and a giant catapult.

Marco's Book

After the captives were freed, their book became wildly popular. People loved reading tales of exotic lands, strange customs, and bizarre animals and food. They shivered through scary stories about the Mongols and the vast deserts. They laughed at the idea of black rocks that burned and paper used as money. But they never really believed that a single word was true. So-called experts were especially quick to dismiss Marco's account.

Milione, which means "million," became Marco's nickname. People used it to tease him. Poor Marco, always on about his life in China: cities greater than any in Europe, an emperor for a friend, golden tablets used for travel, a princess's escort. Who could believe him? Where were his millions now? All he had were a million lies in his book. *Milione*, ha.

Eventually, Marco married and had three daughters. When he tucked his daughters in at bedtime, they loved to hear him tell his stories. At least they always believed the stories were true.

Adventures on the Ancient Silk Road

Marco's Book

Marco used his journals and his memories to dictate his story. Rustichello added bits to make the story more exciting. We have no way of knowing what Rustichello added and what Marco told him.

In a few months, the book spread across what is now Italy. It was soon translated into a dozen other languages. The printing press had not been invented yet, so people copied the text by hand. They also changed the stories, adding some parts and leaving out others. Sometimes they made mistakes too. No two copies of the book were exactly the same. No original manuscript has ever been found, but about 140 different early copies of the book have survived.

In 1324, as Marco lay dying, his friends begged him to admit everything in his book was made up. "No!" Marco answered. "I did not lie. I will not take anything back. I have not written down half of what I saw." He died firm in his claims that everything in his book was true.

Marco Polo traveled through China, around the surrounding countries, and along the Silk Road for 24 years. He was one of the first European travelers to visit China. (The others were religious missionaries: men who tried to convert people to Christianity.) He was the man who introduced China and the Silk Road to Europeans. After he returned home, though, the Mongol peace ended in Asia. Marco's was the last European account of the Far East and the Silk Road that would be written for a long time.

successfully hid their treasures. For example, near the oasis city of Dunhuang were hundreds of caves. Over the centuries, the caves had become Buddhist shrines, decorated with beautiful paintings and statues, sheltering scriptures and other documents. One cave in particular was filled with thousands of documents, kept in good condition by the extremely dry weather. Toward the end of the nineteenth century and in the early years of the twentieth, British and Russian archeologists discovered the caves and many other sites, carting off loads of these priceless treasures. More than 40,000 Asian items collected by Sir Aurel Stein from the lands surrounding the Silk Road are preserved in the British Museum in London, England.

Today the main business of the Silk Roads is not trade but tourism. As in old days, some regions are unsettled and either closed to travel or unsafe. However, many routes are now open. The modern traveler can go by plane, train, bus, car, or bicycle, as well as on horseback, on camel-back, or on foot.

If you make your own journey, you will find a mixture of old and new. The highway through the Pamir Mountains is a triumph of modern engineering; however, there is only a footpath through most of the Wakhan Corridor, which separates the Pamirs from the mountains of the Hindu Kush. In Istanbul (old Constantinople), you can still haggle for silk or jade or carpets at thousands of small shops in the arcades of the Grand Bazaar. In Xi'an (old Chang'an), you can visit the restored Great Wild Goose Pagoda, once home to Xuanzang's precious Buddhist manuscripts. In some of the old slave bazaars, the auction block still stands, a reminder that human beings were once bought and sold.

Pilgrims come to the holy places of their religions, often combining their spiritual journey with one of the thousands of Silk Road tours. In some of these lands, ordinary people live much as they did centuries ago; nomads of the steppes still move their yurts or gers along with their flocks; the winter winds are still ready to freeze noses and cheeks. In rural China, some farmers still raise silkworms and harvest their thread, although much silk production now is mechanized. And those who venture into the Taklamakan Desert may still hear phantom voices calling in the night or see a mysterious, hazy lake in the distance.

In the Silk Road lands, the presence of our three heroes lingers. Here and there are echoes of Xuanzang, Genghis Khan, and Marco Polo: a pilgrim, a warrior, and a merchant who were willing to brave any danger to fulfil their dreams.

Further Reading

To find out more about the Silk Road and the explorers in this book, start by checking out the following books and websites. Please be careful when clicking on links to other sites, and keep in mind that some website addresses may have changed.

The Silk Road

The Silkroad Foundation website includes detailed maps of the Silk Road routes and a chronology of the Silk Road www.silk-road.com/toc/index.html

Mr. Donn and Maxie's PowerPoint series on ancient China includes resources for teachers http://china.mrdonn.org/silkroad.html

KidsPast.com website about the Silk Road www.kidspast.com/world-history/0135-the-silk-road.php

Academic Kids encyclopedia entry on the Silk Road www.academickids.com/encyclopedia/index.php/Silk_Road

Xuanzang

Note: There are a lot of different ways to spell Chinese names in English. For example, *Xuanzang* may also appear as *Hsuan-Tsang* or *Tang-Sanzang*. The *New World Encyclopedia* entry on Xuanzang (listed below) lists some of the many different spellings of his name.

The Silk Road Journey with Xuanzang by Sally Wriggins. New York: Basic Books, 2003.

Ultimate Journey: Retracing the Path of an Ancient Buddhist Monk Who Crossed Asia in Search of Enlightenment by Richard Bernstein. New York: Vintage, 2002.

Xuanzang on the Silk Road by Sally Wriggins www.mongolianculture.com/indomongolian.htm

The Silkroad Foundation: Travels of Hsuan-Tsang: Buddhist Pilgrim of the Seventh Century www.silk-road.com/artl/hsuantsang.shtml

English Translation of Book One of Xuanzang's *Record of the Western Regions* http://depts.washington.edu/silkroad/texts/xuanzang.html

Encyclopedia Brittanica entry for Xuanzang www.britannica.com/EBchecked/topic/274015/Xuanzang

New World Encyclopedia entry for Xuanzang www.newworldencyclopedia.org/entry/Xuanzang

Academic Kids encyclopedia entry for Xuanzang http://academickids.com/encyclopedia/index.php/Xuanzang

Genghis Khan

Note: Some sources spell *Genghis* differently: a few examples are *Chingis* and *Jinghis*.

The Conquests of Genghis Khan by Alison Behnke. Minneapolis, MN: Lerner Publishing Group, 2007.

Genghis Khan: 13th Century Mongolian Tyrant by Enid A. Goldberg and Norman Itzkowitz. New York: Franklin Watts, 2008.

Genghis Khan: Invincible Ruler of the Mongol Empire by Zachary Kent. Berkeley Heights, NJ: Enslow Publishers, 2007.

Genghis Khan's Mongol Empire by Thomas Streissguth. Chicago: Lucent Books, 2005.

The Life & Times of Genghis Khan by Jim Whiting. Hockessin, DE: Mitchell Lane Publishers, 2005.

Encyclopedia Brittanica entry for Genghis Khan www.britannica.com/EBchecked/topic/229093/Genghis-Khan

New World Encyclopedia entry for Genghis Khan www.newworldencyclopedia.org/entry/Genghis_Khan

Academic Kids encyclopedia entry for Genghis Khan http://academickids.com/encyclopedia/index.php/Genghis_Khan

Marco Polo

The Adventures of Marco Polo by Russell Freedman. New York: Arthur A. Levine Books, 2006.

Marco Polo for Kids: His Marvelous Journey to China, 21 Activities by Janis Herbert. Chicago: Chicago Review Press, 2001.

Marco Polo: Overland to China by Alexander Zelenyj. New York: Crabtree Publishing Company, 2005.

Marco Polo's Silk Purse by Gerry Bailey and Karen Foster. New York: Crabtree Publishing Company, 2008.

Who Was Marco Polo? by Joan Holub. New York: Grosset & Dunlap, 2007.

The Silkroad Foundation: Marco Polo and His Travels www.silk-road.com/artl/marcopolo.shtml

Maps of Marco Polo's routes www.hyperhistory.com/online_n2/maptext_n2/mongol1.html

Asia for Educators, Columbia University: Marco Polo in China (1271–1295) http://afe.easia.columbia.edu/china/trad/marco.htm

Encyclopedia Britannica entry for Marco Polo www.britannica.com/EBchecked/topic/468139/Marco-Polo

New World Encyclopedia entry for Marco Polo www.newworldencyclopedia.org/entry/Marco_Polo

Academic Kids encyclopedia entry for Marco Polo http://academickids.com/encyclopedia/index.php/Marco_Polo

Acknowledgements

First, I must acknowledge the support of three people who have stayed committed to this project through years of vicissitudes: without my publisher, Rick Wilks, Annick Press, and my literary agents, David and Lynn Bennett, Transatlantic Literary Agency, this manuscript would not have become a book. A fourth essential person, Dawn Hunter, continued the work when personal problems laid me low. Though we met only once, Dawn caught my passion and used my manuscripts and references to advantage. Editor Barbara Pulling worked with my earlier manuscripts and Barbara Hehner with Dawn's later ones.

Many others helped earlier, notably scholars and librarians at the university of Toronto, especially at Robarts and E. J. Pratt. Through interlibrary loan, U of T researchers borrowed books from other universities. Linda Hutcheon, renowned U of T professor, my decades ago high school English student, and now my friend, directed me to top experts in East Asian studies and the Humanities. However careful I have been, any remaining errors are mine—or Dawn's, though I have vetted her manuscript and have found her work reliable.

My writing group has supported this project throughout its long process. Sylvia Warsh, Heather Kirk, Vancy Kasper, Lorraine Williams, Barb Kerslake, Pat Bishop, and Ayanna Black, thank you for your years of listening, reading, and responding to my work, from its beginnings through its various stages. Above all, you knew this would be an important and much-needed book: your confidence helped me to persevere despite deteriorating health.

Finally, my family has supported my Silk Road book throughout. My husband, Howard Collum, has loved and helped me unstintingly through long periods of being "away," immersed in far-off lands and long-ago times. My children and their spouses have all helped as well, especially Walt Galloway. Walt is the only member of my family who has lived in both China and India; his experience helped me to develop insights not to be found through the most dedicated research. Howard especially but others too have picked up and returned books to various libraries, or have shopped and cooked and run errands for me through periods when the book has absorbed my life, including Walt and Jan Galloway, Noël Macartney and Wayne Hayball, and Glenn Galloway.

Barring miracles, this will be the last book to bear my name. With heartfelt affection and appreciation to you all,

Priscilla Galloway

I came to the stories of the Silk Road travelers much later than Priscilla did. When we met, her careful research and her enthusiasm for the subject drew me in. I knew these were stories I wanted to help her tell. That would not have been possible without all the dedicated people at Annick Press. Even in the hardest times, they kept the road clear and made sure we would finish this journey. And it was a joy to work with our editor, Barbara Hehner: she offered me encouragement and gently helped me to see the bigger picture. I have learned a great deal from working with Priscilla, Barbara, and Annick, and I thank them all very much for the opportunity.

Dawn Hunter

Photo Credits

Index

Afghanistan, 31, 33, 127
Amalfi, 109
antelopes, 83
Arghun, King of Persia, 145, 149
Armenia, 103–104, 118
armor, 54, 55, 93
Ayas, 103–106, 118

Bamiyan, 31–32
Banda, 9–12
bandits, 1–3, 39, 41–42, 150
bazaars, 103, 130–132
bears, 83
Begter, 64, 65, 68–69
Bezeklik Thousand Buddha Caves, 19
Bianchi, 46
Bolgana, Queen of Persia, 145
Borte, 69–71, 72–74, 80–81
Buddhism
    basics, 8
    China, 7, 46–48, 115
    India, 34, 35–37
    monasteries, 32, 34, 35–37
    places of worship, 19, 31–32
    along Silk Road, 22, 29–30
Bukhara, 93–96, 113

camels, 27, 83, 125, 131
caravanserais, 27, 123
catapults, 87
Chabi, Empress, 115
Chang'an, 5, 6–7
Chengdu (Sheng-du), 5–6, 136–137
China
    8th century, 52
    13th century, 113–115
    20th century, 47
    Jin Dynasty, 76, 79–88
    language, 3
    Ming Dynasty, 132
    money, 143–144
    religion, 7, 46–48, 89, 91, 113–115
    silk making, 56–57
    Song Dynasty, 52, 115
    Tang family, 5, 6, 8
    Yuan Dynasty, 115

Christianity, 113–114
Chu'Tsai, 87
city-states, 109
clocks, 36
clothing, 29, 70
Cobinan, 126
coconuts, 148
Columbus, Christopher, 154
Confucius, 4
crocodiles, 142–143

dancing, 29
deserts, 12–13, 133–134
    Gobi, 81–85, 133–135
    Kizilkum, 27–28, 94–95
    Taklamakan, 10–15
dowries, 71–72

elephants, 38, 40, 41–42, 131

falcons, 121, 122
food
    Chinese, 140–141
    Mongolian, 64, 71
    Silk Road, 21, 26, 29
    transportation, 77–78

Gaozong, Emperor, 46
Gaozu, Emperor, 6, 25
Genghis Khan (Temujin)
    achievements, 99–100
    alliances, 72, 74–75, 89–90, 94
    army, 54–55, 58–59, 81, 92–94
    battle tactics, 75–76, 81–88, 92–98
    character, 91, 97
    childhood, 60–62, 64–69
    and China, 76, 79–88
    clan, 64, 71
    death, 99, 101
    in desert, 81–85, 94–95
    family members, 68–69, 80, 92, 99, 145
    father, 60, 62, 72
    as horseman, 64–68
    message systems, 55, 78
    as military leader, 52–55, 58–59, 74
    as ruler, 87, 89–90

and Silk Road, 76–79, 94, 99–100
wife (Borte), 69–74, 80–81
Genoa, 109, 111, 151
gers, 62, 63
Ghazan, Prince, 149
Gobi Desert, 81–85, 133–135
Great Gobi National Park, 83
Great Wild Goose Pagoda, 45, 47
Great Yasa, 89

Harsha, King, 20, 35, 37–38, 51
Hedin, Sven, 14
Hindu Kush Mountains, 40–41, 127–128
Hindus, 37–38
Hormuz, 124
horses, 52, 64–68, 81, 93, 137
houses, 35, 62, 63

India, 34–38, 51, 149
Iron Gates, 30
Islam, 31, 88
Ismoil Somoni Peak, 128
Italy, 109

Jalal, Prince, 91–92, 98
Jalalabad, 34
Jamuka, 73

Kapisa, 32–33
karezes, 17
Kashgar, 130–132
Kato, Shinpei, 101
Keraits, 71–72
Kerman, 121, 122
khans, 25–26
Khotan, 42, 132
Khwarezm, 88–90, 91, 93–94, 97–98
kings, 20
Kizilkum Desert, 27–28, 94–95
Koagchin, 72, 73, 74
Kokachin, Princess, 145, 149
Kubilai Khan, 78
    character, 139
    and horses, 137
    old age and death, 144, 149
    palaces, 136–137
    and Polo family, 113–118, 120, 137–145
    religion, 113–115
    spy network, 136

Kucha, 21–22
Kuraltai, 92, 99

Lake Issyk Kul, 25
Land of Fire, 16
Lanzhou, 9
Lugou (Marco Polo) Bridge, 119

Ma-Po Tofu (recipe), 140–141
Mao Zedong, 47
maps, 134, 154
Marco Polo (Lugou) Bridge, 119
Marco Polo sheep, 129
marriages, 69–70, 146
measurement
    distance, 43, 49
    time, 36
medicine, 127
merchants
    Italian, 107, 109
    Silk Road, 77–78
    Sogdianan, 6, 27
    trade goods, 33, 71, 77–78, 123, 126, 132
    as traders, 110–111, 112–113, 121, 130–132
    Venetian, 107, 112
Merkits, 72–74
message systems, 55, 78, 79
monasteries, 32, 34, 35–37
money, 32, 121, 143–144, 147
Mongol Empire, 97, 112–115
Mongolia, 52, 89, 91
Mongols, 52, 60–62
    armies, 54–55, 73–74
    clans, 58, 60, 71–72, 74–75
    food, 64, 71
    Great Council (Kuraltai), 92, 99
    and horses, 52, 64–68, 137
    language, 87
    trade, 62, 112–113
    weddings, 69–71
mountains
    Hindu Kush, 40–41, 127–128
    Pamir, 127–130
    Snowy, 30
    Tian Shan, 23–24

Nalanda, 36–37
Nepal, 49

oasis kingdoms, 17, 20, 51–52
    Khotan, 42, 132
    Kucha, 21–22
    Turfan (Turpan), 16–20
Ogedei, 80, 92, 99
Omar Khayyam, 29
Otrar, 90, 93
oxen, 122, 123

paizas (paidzse), 114, 147, 149
Pamir Mountains, 127–130
paper money, 144
pearl divers, 149
Pegolotti, Francesco Balducci, 97
Persia, 121–126, 145, 149
Pisa, 109
poems, 29, 59, 138
Polo, Marco, 102–154
    in Ayas, 103–104, 118, 120
    book, 106, 107, 129, 134, 152–153
    childhood, 106–112
    in China, 119, 139–145, 146–147
    in desert, 125–126, 133–135
    education, 110–111, 124
    illness, 126–127
    journals, 121, 151
    and Kubilai Khan, 139–145, 146–147
    language skills, 110, 111, 118
    later life, 152–153
    in mountains, 127–130
    in Persia, 121–126
    sea voyage, 147–148, 149–150
Polo family
    first trip to China, 112–114
    second trip to China, 117–136
    as traders, 110, 112–113, 118, 121, 130
    trip home, 145–147, 147–151
    in Venice, 106–107, 144, 151
pope, 113, 117, 118

rain-rest, 34
Ramusio, Giovanni Battista, 107
recipe, 140–141
Red Sands Desert, 27–28, 94–95
religion
    China, 89, 91, 113–115
    Mongolia, 71, 89, 91
    Silk Road, 31, 88
rhinoceroses, 148–149
robbers, 1–3, 39, 41–42, 150
Rustichello da Pisa, 151, 153

Saiga antelope, 83
Samarkand, 26, 28–30, 88, 96–98, 113, 116
shamans, 71, 91
sheep, 122, 123, 129
Sheng-du (Chengdu), 5–6, 136–137
Shilabhadra, Venerable, 36–37
ships, 124–125
sieges, 87, 93
silk, 55, 56–57
Silk Road
    caravans, 113
    food, 21, 26, 29
    Genghis Khan and, 76–79, 91, 94, 99–100
    improvements, 78–79, 91, 94
    northern route, 9–34
    sea route, 147–150
    southern route, 38–43
    transport animals, 131
    travelers, 77, 79, 112–115
silkworms, 56–57
Singing Sands (Khongoryn Els), 83
Snowy Mountains, 30
Sogdiana, 6, 26, 51–52
Stein, Aurel, 49
Sumatra, 148–149

Taizong, Emperor, 8, 9, 25, 42–43, 44–46
Taklamakan Desert, 10–15
Taliban, 31
Tanguts, 52, 59, 75
Tian Shan Mountains, 23–24
Tibet, 51–52, 142
tigers, 142
Toghril, 71–72, 73
Tokmak, 25
trade goods
    fruit, 77–78, 126
    fur, 71
    ivory, 33
    jade, 132
    turquoise, 122
trebuchets, 87
Tripitaka, 4
Turfan (Turpan), 16–20
Turks, 25

Uighurs, 52
UNESCO, 31

Venice, 106–111, 112

warfare
    Mongol army, 55, 58–59, 92–94
    sieges, 87, 93
    signaling, 55, 58
    tactics, 75–76, 81–88, 92–98
water clocks, 36
water systems, 17
weapons, 54, 87, 110
weddings, 69–71, 146
Western Xia, 52, 58–59, 75–76
women's rights, 89, 146
World Heritage Sites, 31

Xia, Western, 52, 58–59, 75–76
Xuanzang, 3
    childhood, 4–5
    in China, 4–10, 45–49
    death, 48–49
    in desert, 11–15, 27–28
    family members, 4–5
    as fantasy character, 4
    in India, 34–38
    library, 45
    in mountains, 23–24, 30, 40–41
    in oasis kingdoms, 16–22
    as preacher, 29–30
    return home, 38–44
    in Samarkand, 28–30
    as scholar, 35–37, 46, 48
    writings, 35, 48, 49

yaks, 27, 131
yam (messenger service), 78, 79
Yeh-hu, Great Khan of the Western Turks, 25–26
Yinchuan, 76
yurts, 62, 63

Lake Oswego Jr. High
2500 SW Country Club Rd.
Lake Oswego, OR 97034
503-534-2335